Look What
Faith in God
CAN DO!

UNION HILL CHURCH: TWENTY FIVE
YEARS IN THE NEW SANCTUARY

Union Hill Church Congregation

WESTBOW
PRESS®
A DIVISION OF THOMAS NELSON
& ZONDERVAN

WestBow Press books may be ordered through booksellers or by contacting:

WestBow Press
A Division of Thomas Nelson & Zondervan
1663 Liberty Drive
Bloomington, IN 47403
www.westbowpress.com
1 (866) 928-1240

ISBN: 978-1-5127-8461-9 (sc)
ISBN: 978-1-5127-8463-3 (hc)
ISBN: 978-1-5127-8462-6 (e)

Library of Congress Control Number: 2017906738

Print information available on the last page.

WestBow Press rev. date: 05/08/2017

We would like to dedicate this book to Eunice Minton, who came to Toby Smalley back in the late 1990s and asked him to help her put together a history book of the church, and to all of those who have attended Union Hill Church in the past, present, and future.

TABLE OF CONTENTS

Old Sanctuary at Union Hill Church

01/02/2007

New Sanctuary at Union Hill Church

ACKNOWLEDGMENTS

The History Committee

The History Committee would like to thank all the people who participated in the creation of this history book. Whether you wrote a chapter or not, the simple fact that you are or were part of the congregation means that you participated in making this church a great place of worship where God has been able to move. This book was created so that generations to come, if the Lord should tarry, will be able to look back, see what God has done, and hopefully pray that God will either continue or do what He has done again in the history of this church.

God established Union Hill Church in 1921 and seventy years later in 1991, made it possible for a new sanctuary to be built debt free. It is now 2017, and this house of worship is ninety-six years old. In four more years, it will reach its hundredth year. God has been good to Union Hill Church. It has produced pastors, preachers, evangelists, teachers, ministers, and singers. Some have stayed here while God has moved others elsewhere.

This book was not created to bring glory to man's accomplishments but to what God has done using vessels that were willing to work for Him. We give God all the glory for everything He has done!

Sharon Fulton
Bobby Minton
Toby Smalley

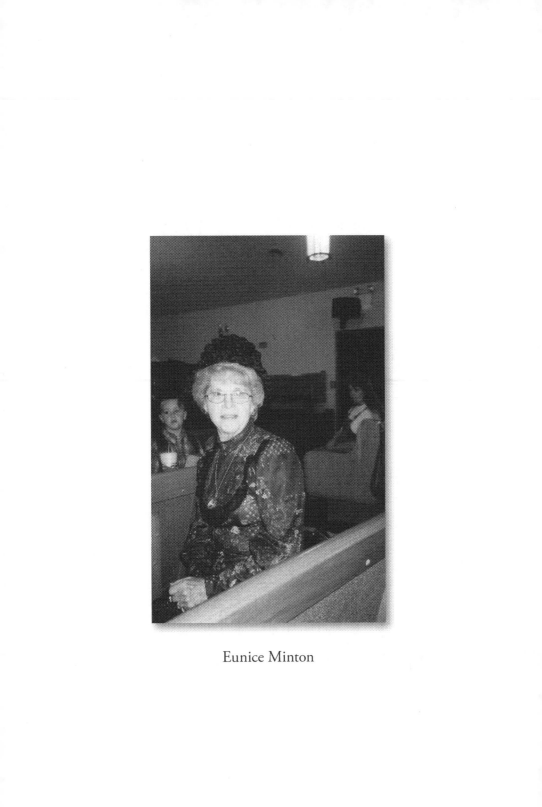

Eunice Minton

INTRODUCTION

Toby Smalley

Twenty-five years ago, on February 29, 1992, the congregation of Union Hill Church moved into its new sanctuary. As you drive north up Union Hill Road from State Route 32, on the left-hand side you will notice a brick building with the name Union Hill Church. There is a covered area at the front entrance where you can drop people off. There are double glass doors that open into the church foyer.

As you walk into the foyer, you see the pastor's office on the left, the sound room on the right, two coat racks, and in front of you on the far side of the foyer, the men's and ladies' restrooms and a nursery. On the right, just past the sound room and one of the coat racks, are the double doors, which open into the sanctuary.

As you go through these doors, you walk into a place of worship. There is burgundy carpet throughout the sanctuary and on the pulpit's platform. The oak pews are covered with rose-mauve colored material.

The sanctuary seats approximately 250 people, including the seats on the pulpit's platform. A podium, two chairs (one for the pastor and one for the leader of the service), and the choir risers are located on the pulpit's platform. Also on the platform are the piano and guitar sections to the right and the drums to the left.

On the back wall behind the choir risers is a mural of Jesus with His hands outstretched. This is a wall we kept from the old church and moved into the new church. Truby Abbott, who was a local artist and preacher, painted it in 1981.

A solid oak altar lines the front of the pulpit's platform and stretches between the two sets of steps that lead onto the platform. This is our house of worship. The church also has a full basement with two bathrooms, a utility room, and Sunday school classrooms.

We welcome all people to our church. We have always been a church where different denominations have come together to worship the Lord.

We believe in the Holy Trinity: the Father, the Son, and the Holy Spirit. We believe that Jesus is the Son of God, who was born of a virgin and died on the cross to shed His blood for the salvation of our souls and the healing of our bodies. We believe in water baptism and in being baptized in the Holy Spirit. We believe in the gifts of the Spirit—wisdom, knowledge, faith, healings, working of miracles, prophecy, discerning of spirits, tongues, and the interpretation of tongues—and that they should be operational in every church service. We also believe what Jesus said in Matthew 22:37–40 (KJV), which says that the greatest commandment is to love God with your whole heart, soul, and mind and that this is the first and greatest commandment. The second is to love others as you love yourself.

This book was written by congregants and officiants of our little church. We wrote it to show our appreciation to God for what He has done and to highlight key events since the building of the new sanctuary. It is our hope that this book will give our future congregation a glimpse of what God has done and can do and inspire them to allow Him to continue to move. In addition, we hope that it will inspire other Christians and churches to honor God and to allow Him to move in their congregations.

THE 1991 REVIVAL

Pastor Phil Fulton

In 1981, I knew we needed more room in our church so the board decided to build a twelve-foot addition to the pulpit area. We also needed more parking spaces so I contacted Gladys Thompson, who owned the property on the north side of the church, and she donated a half acre of ground to the church.

The Holy Ghost was moving in a mighty way. I had been urging the church and our board members to build a new church, not because it was my dream to build it but because the Spirit had spoken to me and said, "It is time to build." We were outgrowing our building. We had to set up extra chairs every service for all the new people.

One, cold Sunday night in January of 1991, a Holy Ghost revival exploded on the Hill. In the following nights, forty-seven precious souls came to the altar. It was a revival like we had never experienced before. Sometimes people came to Christ during the first song and others came midway through the service. Some nights I preached and some nights I didn't. God would move, and people came to the altar and accepted the Lord as their Savior. It was amazing.

It had been standing room only for weeks even after the revival had ended. Then on Easter Sunday in 1991, I saw people come into the church and leave because there was no place to sit or to stand. We needed to build or disobey what God had placed in my heart to do. The board then agreed to build. We brought it before the church, and the church also agreed.

Mr. and Mrs. Irvin Smith had purchased the Thompson property. Mrs. Smith wanted to donate some land to the church. Mrs. Smith had a serious illness that eventually took her life. Before she died, she told her husband to donate the land, but instead, he buried her in the area she wanted to donate, which only left a small area to build on. Mr. Smith told us he would give it to the church. I had the land surveyed, a deed drawn up, and called him to set up a time to sign the deed, but he refused to sign it. Little did we know that God had a better plan and used the devil to fulfill it.

I contacted Mr. Greg Cline, whose mother had attended Union Hill Church as a young girl and had left the property behind the church to her son. I told Mr. Cline we wanted to build a new church and would like to buy some of his land. He said, "No, I don't want to sell any of the land, but I will donate what you need." So he gave the church one and a half acres. Oh, God is so good and provided the perfect spot for our new church.

Pastor Rodney Roark at the Peebles Baptist Church was also a building contractor. He agreed to build the new church and to allow those who were in the church to do much of the work, which saved us thousands of dollars. Our people worked many evenings and every Saturday to get the work done. The ladies of the church fixed dinner on Saturday for all the workers.

We saw God move in miraculous ways while we were building the church. All of the bulldozing services, the paint, and tons of fill dirt were donated. People handed me checks anywhere from a hundred to a thousand dollars at different times during the building project.

Most amazing of all, people had warned me that the church would split during the building project, but as far as I know, there was not even one argument or cross word spoken. We moved into our new church on the last Saturday of February, 1992, *debt free*! I preached from Psalm 150:2 that night. Praise Him for His mighty acts. It truly was the mighty hand of our God that enabled us to do this.

After we moved into our new building and removed the old church, I thought about building a community center where we could have our church dinners and plays and where our young people could get together, but we had no land to build it on. I had enquired about the property across the road, but it had not been for sale.

In April of 1998, I received a call from Cecil and Neisel Palmer. They asked me if we were still interested in buying some of their property. As a result, we purchased nine acres from them, and they donated the purchase price of two acres.

In 2000, we decided to build the community center on the land we had purchased. The men in the church took on this project. I took the purchased the materials and made sure they were delivered. We put in some long hours, but thank God, just ten years after moving into our new church, we opened our brand new $275,000 community center *debt free*! We serve such an awesome God.

In 2003, Greg Cline called me and asked if the church was interested in buying his property. At the time, we didn't have the money and didn't believe in borrowing it from a banking institution. I brought it before our board members. We decided that if we could work out a land contract, we would purchase the property. Mr. Cline was very agreeable to this, and in September 2003, we purchased forty-seven acres and paid it off by January of 2006.

We have experienced great and mighty things in the last twenty-five years. To God be the glory!

1991 REVIVAL

TOBY SMALLEY

One of the greatest events that I have seen at Union Hill Church was the 1991 revival. It took place at the beginning of the Gulf War when our country was worried. This God-sent revival broke loose one Sunday night on January 13, 1991. Pastor Phil Fulton preached, and I led the services. I kept a record of this revival in my Bible. What God was doing was amazing.

This revival led us to build our new sanctuary. If I remember correctly, the old church only seated a hundred people, and it was packed every service. At that time, we had church services on Saturday and Sunday nights and on Sunday mornings, along with Sunday school.

As I said, the church was packed during its regular services. God moved in a mighty way in each one of them. People were getting saved, and then it happened. We had one of the most powerful services I had ever seen. We had been praying for God to save the *lost husbands* of the church, and on that Sunday night, one of them, Keith Spriggs, gave his heart to the Lord. That started a revival that no one has ever forgotten.

In that two-week revival, forty-seven souls were saved. Some nights, Pastor Phil preached, and some nights he didn't. God took over, and people came to the altar for salvation or healing. Our church members sang and shouted, and people were saved. One night, Pastor Phil preached with such an anointing and the conviction was so heavy, I turned to Ronnie Anderson and told him that it made me want to get saved all over again.

The congregation was excited. The services didn't start until 7:00

p.m., but people would begin to arrive at 5:00 p.m. They came prepared for church.

Many times the Spirit began to move when the pianist played before the church service even started. Our pastor preached some of the most anointed sermons we had ever heard. Salvation was the main theme of God's messages, and hell, fire, and brimstone was the result of not receiving salvation.

When God sends a revival, word of it spreads for miles around. Other churches came to visit. People came from the Church of Christ, the Baptist church, the Nazarene church, and many other denominations and independent churches. We worked with them as one body. We had no hindrances in this revival.

I remember on Friday night, January 18, while I was leading the service, the Lord told me that Bobby Purtee was going to walk in the church door and come to the altar. Within a few minutes, the door opened, and Bobby came through the door and to the altar. Wow! What a service!

The following is a nightly documentation, which I wrote in my Bible, of the results from the revival and some of the events during the building of the new sanctuary.

Sunday, January 13, 1991
Revival breaks loose.
Pastor Phil Fulton preached. Toby Smalley led the services.
Four people were saved the first night:
Keith Spriggs
Elizabeth Pendel
Don Smith
Beth Fulton
Brian Fulton came forth to make sure he was saved.

Monday, January 14, 1991
One saved:
Rick King

Tuesday, January 15, 1991
No one saved.

Wednesday, January 16, 1991
War breaks loose in the Middle East. US attacks Iraq. Fear they might attack Israel.
Looking for the Lord to come.
Nine saved:
Amy Young
Alisha Young
Audrey Johnson
Chris Cluxton
Jason Shrivner
Teresa Shoemaker
Mrs. Smith
Shanda Pinkerton
Becky King Smalley

Thursday, January 17, 1991
Seven saved:
Regina "Gina" Smalley
Amy Anderson
Bobby Kent Minton
Wendy VanHoy
Randy Aber
Julie Beth Purtee
Melissa Minton

Friday, January 18, 1991
Four saved:
Ronnie Shriver (got saved at home)
Anita Conaway
Amber Knauff
Bobby Purtee

I was leading the service when the Lord told me that Bobby Purtee was going to come through those doors and get saved. And to my surprise, it came to pass.

Saturday, January 19, 1991
One saved:
Margaret Smith

Sunday Morning Service, January 20, 1991
During Sunday school, seven saved and one recommitted:
Mark Anderson
Don Smith
Don Smith Jr.
Billy Joe Swayne
Lee Shanks
Angie Wood
Robbie Clark
Rick Gaffin (recommitted)

Sunday Evening Service, January 20, 1991
Three saved:
Sandy Jones
Beth (relation to the Lambs)
Jessica Smalley

Monday, January 21, 1991
Verdi Grooms came to the altar. Didn't pray through but still praying. Lord is dealing with Jeff Swayne.

Tuesday, January 22, 1991
Three saved:
Tim Adams
Alice Baird's two daughters
Verdi Grooms came again to the altar but still didn't pray through.

Wednesday, January 23, 1991
Two saved:
John Dixon
Kim Williams
Verdi Grooms still praying.

Thursday, January 24, 1991
One saved:
Verdi Grooms got saved!

Friday, January 25, 1991
No one saved.

Saturday, January, 26, 1991
Two saved:
Tim Howe
Lisa Howe

Sunday Evening Service, January 27, 1991
One saved:
Billy Dale Purtee
Revival ended.
Forty-seven souls saved. Praise the Lord!

After the Revival Was Over
The following were baptized at Burkit Road in Pike County. The baptisms were performed by Pastor Phil Fulton and Ronnie Anderson:
Keith Spriggs
Bobby Purtee
Ronnie Shriver
Don Smith

July 14, 1991

As a result of the revival, seventeen more were baptized. Pastor Phil Fulton, Boyd Young, Brenda Spriggs, and Brenda Smith performed the baptisms:

Gina Smalley

Chris Cluxton

Tim Howe

Lisa Howe

Beth Aber

Randy Aber

Tim Adams

Amy Young

Shanda Pinderton

Wendy VanHoy

Jason Shriver

Teresa Shoemaker

Lee Shanks

Verdi Grooms

Julie Beth Purtee

David Aryie

Brian Fulton

At the July 1991 Annual Business Meeting

The church voted to build the new sanctuary.

Sunday Morning, August 23, 1991

We had a groundbreaking ceremony with the following elders of the church:

Pastor Phil Fulton

First Elder Harley (Bud) Swayne

Trustee Bob Minton

Trustee Troy Smith

Eernal Ward performed the groundbreaking ceremony.

Also present was our contractor, Rodney Roark, pastor of the Peebles Baptist Church.

First Sunday in August 1991
Started building fund offering. It was taken up on the first Sunday of each month. By October 1991, we had $70,000 in the fund.

Saturday, October 19, 1991
Two people we didn't know volunteered to haul fill dirt given to us by Standard Slag. They hauled forty tons a load and hauled six loads, which totaled 240 tons of fill dirt.

December 6, 1991
John Crum donated the paint for the new church.

December 1991
The York family donated funds to finish paying for the furniture in the new church.
Missionary service with Mark Baer preaching.
Philip Lee Swayne was saved.

Monday, February 17, 1992
Carpet laid in new church.

February 22, 1992
Last Saturday night service in old church.
Mike Smith was saved.

Sunday, February 23, 1992
For a while now, Bud Swayne, who was the first elder, had let me lead the services. On Sunday, February 23, 1992, I asked Bud if, since this was the last service in the old church and the next weekend was the first service in the new church, he wanted to lead the services. He said no, he wanted me to lead them. I counted it an honor that I was able to lead these two services.

Saturday, February 29, 1992
It was leap year, and we moved into the new church building on Saturday, February 29, 1992. I led the service, but Pastor Phil Fulton

opened it and later preached. It was a wonderful service. The Lord came in a wonderful way. We had about 270 people in the service from all different denominations. The church would only hold around 250 so we had to set up more seats. That night Roland (Turtle) Wallace was the first person to get saved in the new church.

Sunday morning, March 1, 1992

During the Sunday School church service, God again manifested Himself. There was such a sweet spirit. Eunice Minton said she felt like a millionaire and later sang that song. There were lots of testimonies and hugs. A wonderful service. We never got to the Sunday school classes.

March 8, 1992

At 2 p.m. we had the church dedication service. We had Rev. Curtis Sheets from Grove City, Ohio, come to preach the message that day. The message came from Psalm 127:1 (KJV). Except the Lord build the house, they labor in vain that build it. The message title was "Are You a 2 X 4, a 2 X 6, or a 2 X 8?" God came again in a special way. To God be the Glory!

THE NEW CHURCH

BOBBY MINTON

When a new church was first mentioned, I'll be the first to admit I was not ready to jump on board. As the prospect of this new church moved ahead, Rodney Roarke, then the pastor of the Baptist church in Peebles (also a building contractor), spoke to Pastor Phil about how the Lord had told him there was something he needed to do for Union Hill Church. This set the wheels in motion for the building project.

At our first planning meeting, I said that if it was the Lord's will for the church to be built, the financing would be there and no money would have to be borrowed. Believe me, it was God's will because we never had to borrow one single cent. That's how great He is.

One instance in particular was when Pastor Phil, Ronnie Shriver, and I met with Jerry Huntley at the audio company he worked for in Norwood (suburb of Cincinnati) While there, we agreed on the sound system we would use in the new church. On the way home, Phil was concerned as to whether we had enough money to cover the cost of this sound system, but the Lord, as always, moved in glorious ways. When we returned home, someone gave Phil a check that covered the full cost of the new sound system.

This was just one of the many things that happened during the whole project. There was never a disagreement, and no one got mad if he or she didn't get his or her way regarding a particular color for the carpet or the type of trim, for example. Everyone was in one accord.

God also knew where he wanted the church to sit. Where it sits now is not on the originally planned spot. As they started clearing the land, they opened up one of the most beautiful views in Ohio. There were five of us, I believe, that were there that morning (my father Bob Minton, Bud Swayne, Troy Smith, Lee York, and myself). We all agreed this was where the Lord wanted the church to sit.

I called the architect, John Hortel, and asked him if it would be possible to move the church to this new location. He assured us that it would be no problem. As you look out from the west windows, you can see why the Lord wanted the church to sit where it is. When you gaze over the beautiful valley beyond, you see the glorious creation of God.

We moved into our beautiful new church debt free. This is a wonderful testimony of what God does for His people when we're in His will. I could go on with many more examples, but these, I believe, were a few of the miraculous things that took place during this exciting time in the building of our new church.

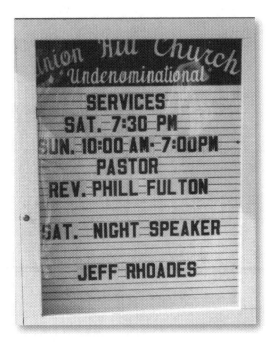

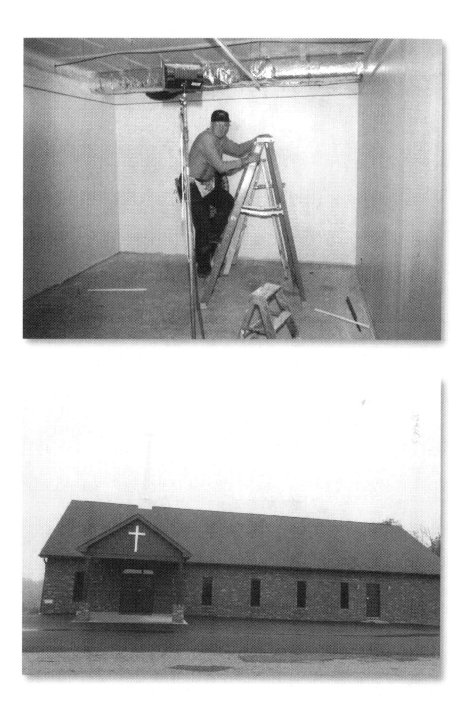

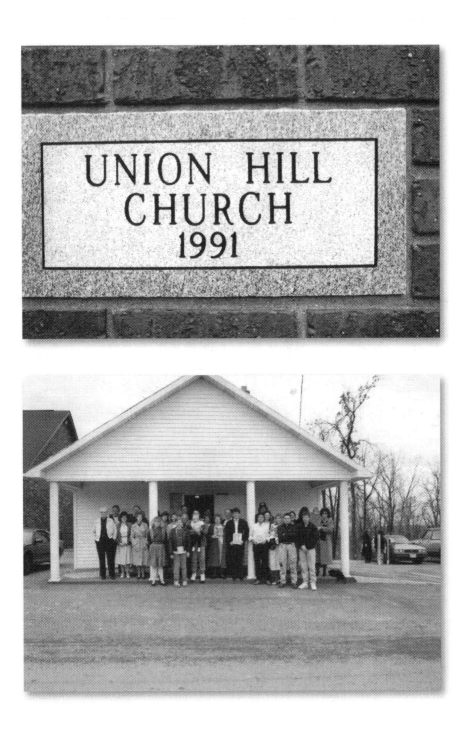

Building the new church

WELCOME

DEDICATION SERVICE

March 8, 1992

SPECIAL SINGING by the CHOIR:
My Tribute (To God Be the Glory)
I've Got a Feeling
   Soloist: Phil Swayne
Look What the Lord has Done
   Soloist: Judy Ann Ward
He's Still in Business

Comments & Recognitions...Rev. Phil Fulton

Prayer...................Rev. Rodney Roark
          Pastor of Peebles Baptist Church

Dedication Address.......Dr. Curtis Sheets
     Pastor of Pleasant Grove Baptist Church
                         Grove City, OH

SPECIAL THANKS

     To Mr. and Mrs. Greg Cline for donating
the land for the new church. To the Local
Businesses and Individuals who have donated
greatly to our work. To our own people who
have donated countless hours of their time
and finances. Also to the Ladies of the
Church for their delicious meals on Saturdays.
To our Contractor, Rev. Rodney Roark and to
our Architect, John Hortel. To Dr. Curtis
Sheets and his congregation for praying diligently for our Building Project. We couldn't
begin to name all who have helped and supported us. Our many thanks to you.
To God be the Glory.

Psalms 127:1 Except the Lord build the house,
             they labour in vain that build it.
Psalms 126:3 The Lord hath done great things
             for us; whereof we are glad.

45

BRIEF HISTORY OF THE UNION HILL CHURCH

The Union Hill Church was founded in December 26, 1921, when Rev. Meredith Palmer deeded the ground the church was built on. The church was in the Council of the Church of Christ in Christian Union.

Some of our former Pastors were: Chris VanMeter, Johnny Anderson, Meredith Palmer, Orval Spence, Russell Kopeck, Mack Knisley, Paul Ferguson, George Belcher, Autumn Scott, Jim Oiler, Pete Kiser, Paul Marhoover.

In 1964, the church voted to go Independent and withdrew from the Council of the Church of Christ in Christian Union. At the time we paid the Council $1000.00 for the church building and became known as The Union Hill Undenominational Church. Our Pastors from that time have been: Carey Hilterbran, Roy Willis and our present Pastor, Phil Fulton. Phil became pastor in July, 1975.

The church has been the birth-place of many preachers and several pastors have their spiritual roots here. We have been a church to worship with all denominations.

Many of the beginning members such as the Swaynes, Hilterbrans, Thompsons, and Wards still have families that attend here.

Our greatest goal is to see people saved and we hope that this bigger building that seats 250 will help to accommodate many new souls.

You are welcome to attend any or all of our services: Saturday 7:30 P.M. Sunday 10:00 A.M. and 7:00 P.M.

Bulletin of Dedication Service

THE MAKING OF THE ALTAR

TOBY SMALLEY

As construction of the church proceeded, a discussion began as to what type of altar the church would have. It was determined that the altar would be funded by donations only. It would not take up a lot of room but would be the focal point in the church. It would match the rest of the woodwork. We agreed that it needed to be the same height as the platform. In addition, it needed to be flush with the front of the platform and occupy the entire length between the two sets of steps. It also needed to have two boards on top with routed edges.

It was constructed with only four boards. The front was constructed with two solid, white oak boards, which were approximately two inches thick, twelve inches wide, and fifteen feet long. One was stacked on the top edge of the other, creating a twenty-four-inch-tall facial board. The top was constructed with two white oak boards, which were one inch thick, eight inches wide, and fifteen feet long. One was placed on top of the other, making the top approximately two inches thick. The top board was trimmed to six and a half inches wide and a routed edge was applied.

Over two thousand dollars was raised to fund the material for the construction of the altar. Harley (Bud) Swayne knew the owner of Willis Lumber Company in Washington Court House, Ohio. Harley, Bobby Minton, and I went there and purchased just the right materials. The company shipped the materials to the new church and carried them inside where my wife and I were installing the altar.

My wife sanded and varnished the altar. I first fastened the two-inch boards by gluing the edges together and crawling under the platform and fastening the boards to the front frame of the platform. I then put the top boards on so that they overlapped the top edge of the face boards and then glued and fastened them from underneath the platform. This way the fasteners did not show on the altar.

It was amazing what God did. These boards never had any flaws. Though they were heavy and unbendable, we attached them without any problems, and the front was seamless. To God be the Glory.

Led out in prayer by Phil Fulton

Led out in prayer by Phil Fulton

Information building on Aug 26, 1991
Present were Earnee Ward, Bud Swayne, Tom Smith,
Keith Ward, Ronnie Anderson, Troy Smith, Bobby Minton,
Lee York, Larry Swayne, Phil Fulton and contractor
Rodney Roark, Sharon Fulton & Judy Ward

Rodney explained building project from ground
up Union Hill is going to do plumbing and
heating

Tony Meadows, framing contractors Waynesville
5/8 plywood for roofing. Not going to put steps
out on ends of pulpit, going to move them in.
Earnee would like to do the oak trim
$158,373.60 —
Cost plus 10% over cost of total job
$2000. savings if we paint
Clean up - savings
Any place Rodney saves - Union Hill saves
A. Solid bid - figure higher for overruns.
B. Cost plus 10%
put account in Union Hill Church - no taxes

Vinyl siding and vinyl soffit
shingles, siding, paint, carpet, brick

$4000. floor coverings (not basement)
$2500. Cross + steeple (steeple $300 crane labor)

most questionable - lumber
electrical contr - Ed Cross
Lights auditorium -
$20,000.00 HVAC - plumbing bid $5000.00 · $15,000.00 auditorium furniture seats
400 amp service   198,000.
parking lot finished job - nearly $200,000.00

49

Called Irvin Smith Aug 26, 1991, Phil, Keith, Rodney Roark, Final — Smith said no decided to go on without his land. God surely had something better in mind.

Rodney Roark 1-695-0129 Winchester
" " Church Peebles 587-3175

Rodney is not figuring any work Union Hill does, Paul Rauthwell, parking lot.

Estimate about January we will be in our new church.

Paul Rauthwell will start Aug 27 on Tuesday.

Painting in front, do it by the hour. Rodney will not guarantee it to get in the new church. Picture up front (of Jesus)

If it holds frames up it will cost extra, Crane will cost extra.

2x6 cross ways every foot - screw in wall. If its possible Union Hill will help in any way.

Trim windows. Do painting - Maybe siding.

If we pay framers $1000.00 we pay Rodney $700.00   Cost + 10%

No fire alarms Counted $3000.00 alarms Use $100,000.00 probably in the end of Nov.

Framers stay in basement of church Mon Thru Friday. Need phone for Workers at church!

Bible stand not over $600.00

Meeting John Clark, Keith Ward,
Phil Guitow, Earnel, Bud, Troy, Tom S.,
Walt, Larry Joe, Bobby M.

Recieved blue print back from state.
additional fee $141.00 — owe to John Hortel
certificate for plan approval
{ 15 in footers / foundations, roof,
exterior wall - approved
burglar alarm - $3000.00
plumbing permit - recieved
Rodney R. talked to building inspector
about moving church - said shouldn't be no
problem.
Everything approved but electrical, heating
and air conditioning

Man doing electric will come and meet
Union Hill men, show lights & explain work
A. Couple changes, change doors from end to
back - going to use our own double doors
upstairs - no retaining wall needed on side
use our doors & save $2200.00.
B. stairstepping wall on side
{ Move church 8 foot towards road - (yes) agreeable
{ New church will be only about 3 ft from
old church.
discussed where to put system 5000 gals - $1300.00

Hoping to frame end wall?
Gable ends - siding or brick whole end.
Brick on both ends gables $1500. each $3000 more

Monday Aug 26, 1991

Had first meeting with Rodney Roark. Measured off new building on right hand side of church. Rodney went over contract, discussed building procedures. Paul and Dale Rothwell, were also there. They are going to do our dozing.

Tuesday Aug 27, 1991

Paul and Dale Rothwell brought in dozers. They begin moving stumps and clearing off area on right side of church and behind. Our contractor and dozer workers decided church would be better on left side of church! They cleared it off. Took down trees on left side of church. Rodney Roark was present. Ordered phone $180.04

Wednesday Aug 28, 1991

Dozer work was finished up this day. Rodney Roark was present

Thursday Aug 29, 1991 (Rodney was present)

Doze equipment taken out. Ronnie Shriver brought in grader and delivered 5 loads $303.24 of stone which he donated to Union Hill Church.

Friday Aug 30, 1991

Clyde Pertinat brought in backhoe and finished digging out wall of basement. He charged $300.00. Rodney was present.

Sat Aug 31, No Work
Mon Sept 2   "   "
Tues Sept 3   "   "
Wed   "   4 "   " rained
Thurs   5   "   " rained
Friday - 6 Men started laying up footer.

installing Trusses for sound room about $400 in loft. 12'x6'x6'

1 way mirror nursery $300.00 3'x5ft

$2000. labor painting, he furnishes paint —

Contract — went over with men — all trustees signed 4 sets — 2 for us — 2 for Rodney
Check for material & labor it's Cost + 10%

Septic System — Men going to try to bury and take care of this

John Hortel
(614) 775-7435

102 Trout Hill Dr.
Chillicothe Ohio 45601

9/3/91 Check to John Hortel $141.00

Ray Greene
Box 10927 St Rt. 28W
New Vienna Ohio 45159
ph 987-2272

54

Sat Sept 7, 1991 - Ron Anderson, Keith Spurges,
Keith Ward, Jim Howe, Tom Smith, Bobby Wrenton,
Toby Smalley took siding off back of church.
Put liquid nail down every 2x4 on back
of painting on outside. Put up plyboard for
outside wall. Rodney was present.
Paid Rodney $808.00
   Mon Sept 9, 1991   rained
   Tues Sept 10 - footer was poured. Rodney
was present. It sprinkled this day.
   Wednesday Sept 11 - Rodney came to church
at 8:30 A.M to check on footer and was back
at 6:00 P.M. Phone Co. installed service today
at noon. Rodney said everything looked fine
   Thurs. Sept 12 - Started putting up forms
for basement. Rodney was present.
   Friday Sept 13 Finished pouring walls
today. Rodney was here all day. Had a
meeting this night with Jerry Burress
about our pews, carpet, and lights. Our
carpet, pile $9.20 installed, plush $10.00
installed, lights $155.00 p/h included.
Pews $14,300.00. Down payment 30% = $4,290.00
Rodney was present.
   Sat. 14, Larry Swayne & boys from church
put in rough plumbing in floor of new
church, before cement was poured. Rodney
was present.
   Mon 16, 1991 - Wall pourers took down (Rodney)
walls this day. paid them $1000.00 uptown same
Tuesday 17, 1991 Inspector came this
day
   Wednesday 18 - Larry Joe Swayne, needed men
from church to put clean out drain in

55

pipes Worked all evening.
Thursday 19, 1991

Friday - 20, 1991 - System delivered, floor poured.
Sat 21, 1991 Men from church put iron frame
on back of picture, etc. Rodney present
Sept 30, Mon delivered cement blocks. Rodney present
Oct 1, Block layers Worked this day, left about
1:00 ran out of water.
Oct 2, Wednesday. Rodney brought up water
tank, block layers worked.
Oct 3 Thursday Block layers worked, finished
up this day.
Oct 7 - No Work - Bobby + Phil hauled gravel.
Oct 8 Tues Haas delivered lumber today
for framing of church. Framers from
Waynesville came today Stayed in basement.
Oct 9 Wed framers worked today
Oct 10 Thurs Framers worked today
Oct 11 Friday framers worked today. They
went back home for the weekend
Oct 12 Sat Rick Jr put water in cistern.
Dug out for septic tank Larry Joe borrowed
back hoe.
Oct 14 Mon. Framers returned Staying in
basement
Oct 15 - Tues. Framers worked
Oct 16 Wed Framers worked
Oct 17 Thurs. Crane came today to move
picture out of old church and into new church.
Crane came at 1:25 — 2:00 had picture hooked
onto crane. Picture was moved without a
problem. Crane also put rafters on new building

56

for framers. Put up wall in back of old Church. Women that made supper for workers. Crane charged Ronnie $41.00 for moving picture.

Oct 18 Friday, Septic tank delivered today. Cost $600.00. Crane finished up today Cost $690.00 - Charged $60. hr

Oct 19 Sat. Hauled in tons of gravel for fill in behind new Church. Larry Joe hooked up septic tank.

Oct 21, Monday. Framers worked.
" 22 Tues. Framers worked
23 Wed. Framers worked
24 Thurs Framers worked
25. Fri Framers finished up.

Oct 26 Sat. Our men worked. Earnel & men put up basement walls.

28, Mon. Electricians worked - Parker Glass started putting in windows.

29 Tues Electricians worked.

30 Wed - Electricians worked. Larry Joe & crew worked.

31 Thurs. Electricians worked. Larry Joe & crew worked.

Nov 1 Friday Electricians worked Larry Joe & crew worked. Steeple delivered & damaged Brick delivered.

Nov 2 Sat. Our men worked on cold air return Men hauled in carpentry sand for brick.

Nov 4 - insulators worked ¬ revival - cold

Nov 5 insulators worked - revival - brick workers'

Nov 6 insulators worked - revival brick workers

Nov 7 revival -

57

dry Wallers Worked

Nov 9 - Sat. Our men Worked on plumbing.

Nov 10 - dry Wallers Worked

Nov 12 - dry Wallers Worked - brick workers
   Worked

Nov 13 - - brick workers worked

Nov 14 - More brick delivered - Brick workers
   worked today.

Nov 15 - dry Wallers

Nov 16 - Our men worked on plumbing with
Larry Joe - hauled in fill gravel

Nov 18 - Parker Glass hung doors - Earnel &
Keith took down old church doors -
John Chamblain worked on soffit.
Siding & soffit delivered.

Nov 19 Tuesday

Nov 20 Wed - Larry Joe & his men worked
on electric & plumbing. Our men went out that
night and worked too.

Nov 21 Thurs

Nov 22 Friday - rained - bricker worked - brick was
delivered - Toby, John Chamblain worked at church

Nov 23 Sat. Our men worked on ele & plumbing
with Larry Joe - Brickers worked - Our men hauled
   in fill dirt.

Nov 24

Nov 25

Nov 26

Nov 27 - Our men helped Larry Joe

Nov 28 - Thurs - Thanksgiving - Brick layers
worked - bricked up end of new church
Nov 29 Friday Our men put up siding &
soffit. Men worked on plumbing and electric.
Brickers worked too.
Nov 30 Sat. Our men worked on siding &
soffit, electric & plumbing. Brickers worked
Dec 2 - Mon - Rodney called & said to
call phone co to move phone

Dec 3 Tues

Dec 4 Wed - Our men worked on
plumbing & electric.

Dec 5 - Dry Wallers are working on ceiling.
John Chamblain & Bud Swayze worked on
soffit.

Dec 6 Friday

Dec 11 Wed - Finish paying brick layers
today. Cross electric worked today. Dry wallers
worked today. Rodney was at Church
Dec 14 Our men worked on plumbing & heating
today.
Dec 20 - Gutter men put up gutters. Electricians
worked.

Dec 21 Sat. Our men worked on plumbing +
electric
Dec 23 no one worked
Dec 24 no one worked
Dec 27. Our men worked on plumbing
+ electric, drywallers worked. Eunice,
Teddy, Judy Ann put first coat of
paint on sanctuary. Ronnie + Bobby
hauled stone.
Dec 28 Sat. Our men worked on
water lines. Jeff primered foyer.
Dec 30 Monday

Dec 31 Tuesday.

Jan 1 Wed Sharon primered office. Our
men worked on plumbing + heating

Jan 2 Thurs. Judy Ann, Eunice, Sharon,
Darlene, Angie, John Clark painted sanctuary,
foyer nursery final coat. Our men
worked on plumbing + heating today.
Lee + Bud Swayne primered block walls
in basement. Larry Joe had his men
work. Ronnie + Bobby spread sand on
cistern. It was cold + rained. Received Steeple!
Jan 3. Lee primered block walls in
basement.

60

Jan 4. Sat. Our men worked on plumbing & heating. Lee primered walls & put up tract for dropped ceiling.

Jan 6 Monday. Lee & Bud Swayne worked on dropped ceiling tract in basement. Drywallers worked about 1 hr. Keith & Judy Ann stained trim & varnished some. Rodney was present. Keith cut hole in attic. Joly stained altar
Jan 7 -

Jan 8. Wed - Our men worked on plumbing

Jan 11 - Sharon, Judy Ann, Beth Ann painted block walls in basement. Our men put up steeple today. Our men also worked on plumbing.

Jan 13. Mon Phil laid off this week Martin laid off this week. Drywallers worked.
Jan 14 Tues. Phil primered fellowship hall today.

Jan 15 - Drywallers & mudders finished up today. Phil put first coat paint on fellowship hall. Linda P. & Judy Ann & Martin primered all class rooms & rest rooms in basement. Lee & Bud worked on dropped ceiling. Otto H. helped clean up dirt & dust.

Bud fell on ice.

Jan 16 Earnel & Stella worked on doors.
Martin & Judy Ann painted & primered
upstairs & baths (windchill -25°)
Electric men worked. Lee was not here.
Eunice put 2nd coat on fellowship room.

Jan 17 - Linda P. & Martin, Judy Ann
painted rooms 1 coat paint. Lee
worked on dropped ceiling. Robie & Otto
helped Earnel on doors.

Jan 18 Sat. Our men worked
painted put second coat of downstairs
worked on drop ceiling.

Jan 20 - Martin, Judy Ann, Linda
put second coat paint on everything
else left. Martin tore out coat
racks; he mudded walls & also
worked on door going down stairs.
Eunice, Trudy, Angie, Beth cleaned
lights, windows. mopped upstairs
bathrooms. Age laid tile in baths &
entry down stairs.

Jan 21 Tues. Stella stained doors.
Lee worked on ceiling tracks. Our men
worked this night on plumbing.

Jan 22 Stella stained

Jan 23 Lee started putting up ceiling.
Stella worked & Earnel

Jan 24 Lee worked

Jan 25 Our people worked, cleaned
& moved the cement

Date	Description	Amount
3/5/91	Carroll McKinney deeds Smith	25.00
5/24	Wallingford survey	350.00
7/1	Carroll McKinney deeds	80.00
8/3	Treasure of State	953.95
8/3	John Hostel architect	1800.00
9/3	" " plans back to Col.	141.00
9/7	Rodney Roark 10%	808.00
9/9	Parker Glass	5000.00
9/9	Jerry Burress cross	1475.00
10/1	" " pews	4290.00
9/16	John Mc Hanes	7000.00
9/16	Rodney 10%	700.00
9/20	Don Bartley floor labor	975.00
9/20	Rodney Roark common labor	175.00
9/20	" " 10%	115.00
9/23	Plum Run	952.62
9/30	Valley Paving, sand	35.03
10/1	A1 Church furn, carpet	1286.65
10/1	Plum Run	976.80
10/3	Tom Finney, Block layer	423.00
10/3	Dave Perry " "	423.00
10/3	Kent Self	423.00
10/3	Rodney Roark	412.27
10/7	Lites	373.08
10/10	Plum Run	7599.35
10/10	Haas	604.44
10/11	Rodney Roark	588.00
10/16	Senco, nails	271.62
10/17	Scioto Valley Precasting septic	600.00
10/19	Cassidy Crane	690.00
10/25	Cross Electric	4010.00
10/25	B. J. Development	11000.00
10/25	Action Builders	1200.00
10/25	Rodney Roark	1708.00

Date	Description	Amount
10/29	Haas	$23,119.28
10/30	Plum Run	6.12
10/30	Heritage Insur. Builders	160.00
	Bulldozing	1.00
10/30/91	Total	$ 80,651.21
10/31	Cross Electric	8020.00
10/31	Parker Glass	4500.00
10/31	Rodney Roark	3513.00
11/1	Portsmouth Cement & Lime Co	3112.75
11/1	A. Furn. lights	1860.00
11/1	Rodney Roark	498.00
		$ 102,154.96

Total spent $102,154.96

Date	Description	Amount
11/4	Bill Smalley	100.00
11/4	Barnett Brass & Copper	87.97
11/4	D & D Metal Supply	590.23
11/4	Larry Swayne	1367.25
11/5	Larry Joe Lutes	1597.98
11/8	Hanson Insulation	1266.00
11/8	Ohio Valley Security & Fire	500.00
11/13	Swayne Heating	1483.41
11/13	John Hartel	250.00
11/15	Dave Perry	1200.00
11/15	Tom Ferry	1200.00
11/15	Ohio Valley Dry Wall	3000.00
11/15	Brick	1356.88
11/15	Rodney Roark	853.00
11/18	D & D Metal Larry J.	674.56
11/18	Larry Jo Lennix	2684.00
11/18	John Blankenship	100.00

11/19	Ray Greene, siding	1950.00
11/19	Portsmouth Lime Co, brick	825.40
11/23	Jeff Warfe	100.00
11/26	Highland Plum Run	97.35
11/27	Lykins Gas	166.10
11/30	Dave Perry	810.00
11/30	Tom Finney	800.00
11/30	Rodney Roark	448.00
12/1	#	125,643.09
12/5	septic risers	82.00
12/5	Larry Joe plumbing	1061.50
12/9	Standard Laforge Limestone	50.25
12/9	Haas	2682.69
12/9	D & D Metal Supply	161.89
12/9	Hedges & Co	31.61
12/9	Lutes	1496.92
12/9	Larry Joe	111.00
12/10	Dave Perry	1000.00
12/10	Tom Finney	1000.00
12/10	Rodney Roark	408.00
12/10	Cross Electric	2000.00
12/10	Rodney Roark	200.00
12/11	Cross Ele	976.76
12/11	Drywall	2000.00
12/11	Rodney R.	298.00
12/14	Highland Plum	324.87
12/14	Parker Glass	3000.00
12/19	Cross Ele	4010.00
12/19	Rodney R.	607.00
12/30	Bishops Gutter	482.75
12/30	Ferrell Gas	617.60
	#	147,245.93

		$147,245.93
1/6	Jim Cruea, 4 hr backhoe	120.00
1/6	Hedges & Co Larry Jo	7.89
1/6	Highland & Plum Run	288.50
1/6	" " "	29.70
1/6	D & D Metal Larry Joe	236.97
1/6	Ace Hardware	15.60
1/6	Haas	204.58
1/7	Drywallers	600.00
1/9	Lutes Larry	1409.00
1/9	Hanson Insulation	2552.00
1/13	Jerry's Music	1500.00
1/15	Drywallers	3020.00
1/15	R. Roark 10%	664.00
1/16	Dollar Store paint	61.06
1/18	Standard Loforge	622.53
1/18	Joe Smith dozing	180.00
1/27	Larry Joe labor & supply	532.00
		$159,289.76
1/30	septic tank risers	44.00
1/30	Azz Roark, basement carpet	3501.60
2/1	Joe Smith dozing	45.00
2/4	sweeper	249.95
2/5	1gal paint	18.99
2/5	Security & Fire	1883.00
2/5	McCoy Lumber	36.00
2/5	Haas	1393.57
2/8	Rodney Roark	684.00
2/8	Lutes	1700.14
2/8	Larry Joe	2748.00
2/10	Gas new Church	77.60
2/10	EPH	323.60

4/3 Jerry Huntly PA System   2500.00
4/3 Ed Cross   477.65
2/9 A1 Furn & Carpet   3141.19
3/20 Rodney Roark   367.48
3/20 Rodney Roark   46.00
3/20 Dumas Co. pews   9706.00
3/24 Larry Joe   396.00
3/11 disk office   165.39
      Total   188,694.62

~~2/3 Cross Elec extras~~   ~~477.65~~
~~2/4 furn & carpet~~   ~~3~~

Judy Ann Ward's diary describing the construction of the new church

67

Pastor Phil and Sharon Fulton

MY INTRODUCTION
TO UNION HILL

Pastor Phil Fulton

My introduction to Union Hill Church came in 1965 when I was a young nineteen-year-old pursuing a black-haired girl, whose family attended there. It was in this little, white church, known as the "Lighthouse on the Hill," that the Spirit of the Lord began to deal with my heart.

A year and a half later, Sharon (Teady) Swayne and I were married. The next month, on a Thursday night in October of 1966, a bald-headed, Pentecostal preacher by the name of Henry Hopkins was preaching a revival on the Hill. I went to the altar and was saved. A few months later, Sharon was saved, and we dedicated our lives to serve Jesus Christ and the church He had placed us in.

There were no other young Christians in the church at this time so the older Christians took us under their wings and encouraged us. Sometimes I thought they pushed us to testify, sing, and pray. I didn't understand, at the time, why they pushed us so hard to participate in the services, but these saints of God knew what we needed to grow in the things of God and His word.

As time passed by, my father-in-law, Harley (Bud) Swayne, had me lead the service and the singing time. The Spirit of the Lord began to move in my life in a wonderful way.

The church made me a Sunday school teacher for the teenagers. Later, I was elected secretary-treasurer. I also served on the board of trustees for many years.

Around 1970, the Lord began to deal with my heart about preaching the Word. It was in a revival with Brother Alex Hamilton from Maysville, Kentucky, that God spoke to my heart in a way I will never forget and called me to preach His Word. I didn't accept the call that night but ran from it for a year or so. I finally got so miserable I gave up and accepted the call of God in my life.

When I accepted the call to preach, our church had been going through some trying times. At the annual business meeting, the members failed to elect a pastor. A few weeks later, Reverend Carey Hilterbran, a former pastor and member of the church, started preaching.

Brother Carey taught me many things about the ministry and the Word of God. I copastored with Brother Carey from 1973 to 1974. I was elected as the church's pastor in July of 1975.

When they elected me as their pastor, I thought my heart was going to beat out of my body. My mind said, *God, I didn't sign up for this, and these people don't know what they are doing.* Yet when they asked me if I would accept, I stammered, "Yes."

From that time on, I began to pray, study, and seek God's direction for Union Hill Church. The first few years, we didn't see many souls saved, but when the people came together and prayed for revival, God began to move.

Sharon and I started a monthly Bible study for the young married couples of the church and would rotate to different homes every month. As a result, God blessed us and we grew closer to the Lord and to one another. In the following years God continued to move in marvelous ways that lead up to the 1991 revival and the building of our current sanctuary and where we are today. To God be all the glory.

MY LIFE AT UNION HILL

SHARON FULTON, PASTOR'S WIFE

Train up a child in the way he should go; and when he
is old he will not depart from it.

—Proverbs 22:6 KJV

I was raised in a little, country church called Union Hill Church.
Many referred to it as "The Great Speckled Bird," which is a reference
to a gospel song. Union Hill Church was always a place where many
denominations came to worship. In my teenage years, it became an
independent church so that all faiths could worship, especially those
that believed in the baptism in the Holy Ghost. Granny Swayne, my
grandmother, the first elder, and a pillar of the church at that time, said
she wanted the church to have the freedom of the Spirit.

Just out of high school, I married a local boy. He went to a Methodist
church and didn't quite know what to think of the little country church
on the hill. However, the more he went to church with me, the more he
liked the upbeat music and clapping. He soon gave his heart to the Lord
and was sold out in serving Him. Later, he became the pastor of Union
Hill Church. I knew the Lord was dealing with him about preaching
because the Lord was also dealing with my heart and preparing me
through dreams.

As a teenager, I began to play the piano. This had been a dream of
mine. I would literally dream of playing the piano. My mother had said
she wanted her girls to take piano lessons but she didn't drive. Dad was
always busy on the farm. Even in the winter months he was butchering.

So Mom didn't have a way to get me to piano lessons. She has told me many times how she would pray for her girls to learn to play the piano. Mother loved music, and her family had taught themselves how to play musical instruments. Mother was also a prayer warrior.

Over the years, the church had many ups and downs. However, my husband and I kept holding on and being faithful to the church, which was something my granny and my dad had taught me to do. Dad had been a strong pillar in our church and later became the first elder, a position he held for many years. He wasn't a preacher but always had a scripture and would expound on it.

My husband, Phil, became the pastor in 1975. He was dedicated to seeing the Spirit move and the church grow. In 1991, God brought a mighty revival to Union Hill Church, and many were saved. The church couldn't hold all of the new people, so we began to build a new church, which had been a vision of my husband's for several years. In God's time, that vision became a reality.

God answered my mother's prayer. Since I was a teenager and for fifty-two years, I have been the church pianist. I have also served as a Sunday school teacher and Bible school director and teacher. God has blessed our church tremendously.

MY ASSOCIATION WITH UNION HILL CHURCH

Dr. Curtis Sheets

My Association with Union Hill Church began over thirty-six years ago. Pastor Phil Fulton called me to come and preach at the church. When I arrived on a Saturday night, the church was packed. A brother by the name of Bud had saved me a seat near the pulpit. After the service, Pastor Fulton asked me to return for their revival meetings. This was held in the old church.

We had a great revival. Each night, Brother Bud saved me a seat so I could sit next to the pulpit. Some construction work had been done behind the pulpit before the revival. One night during the revival and as the Lord and I got together, I almost fell into a hole behind the pulpit. That's how I began my association with Union Hill Church.

Pastor Fulton granted me the honor of preaching the dedication service for the new church. Mrs. Sheets and I arrived at around one-thirty or so in the afternoon after I had preached at my own church. When we arrived, the church was packed. After I completed my message and began the dedication, the congregation held hands and made two circles around the sanctuary. We all offered dedication prayers for the building. Brother Fulton and his wife knelt in the center of the sanctuary and completed the dedication prayer.

I was astonished that the entire church, all the furniture, and everything else were paid for. After this, I preached a revival each year at Union Hill Church.

I would like to share some memories that Mrs. Sheets and I experienced over the years.

Sister Eunice Minton

She led the congregational singing. This was how she set the stage for a spiritual service.

Sister Faye Thompson

She sang "Ain't No Grave Gonna Hold My Body Down." The longer she sang, the louder she became and the harder she beat on the pulpit.

Black-Haired, Black-Eyed Girl

My wife and I well remember a little black-haired, black-eyed girl, who sat on the left side of the pulpit and played a tambourine. My wife and I observed this little girl grow up at Union Hill Church. She was always on her feet hopping up and down during the revival. She was always telling people they needed Jesus and was thanking God for keeping the deer out of her way to and from each church service.

Brother Hershel Beavers

We also remember Brother Hershel Beavers. When he sang, he would stick one leg out. We often wondered how he could sing while standing on just one leg.

Brother Toby

I always knew that when Brother Toby Smalley took a running spell something good was about to happen.

Brother Fulton

My wife and I have always been amazed how Brother Fulton knew every song that the congregation sang and sang every word with them.

I thank God that over these past thirty-six-plus years, Union Hill Church has never changed. It still preaches the Gospel, stands for the fundamentals of the faith and against liberalism and modernism, and promotes the cause of Christ.

The new fellowship building. Construction began
in 2000 and finished in 2001 debt free.

Union Hill Church

Directory

UNION HILL CHURCH

1964 Union Hill Road

Peebles, Ohio 45660

Phone # 513-588-2305

Address and phone directory

GOD HAS MOVED!

Betty Shriver

As I was asked to write about the last twenty-five years at our church, I wondered, *What can I say?* Well, a lot has happened over the span of time that I have been a member.

I was born and raised in this church we call Union Hill. From the time I was a baby and on up until I married, my mom made me go to church. That was all I ever knew. I didn't like that my mom had that rule about church, at the time, but as I look back, I am so grateful for this heritage, which has made me what I am today.

I was saved in December of 1974. It was almost midnight before church ended that night, but I knew the exact moment that the Lord came into my soul. It was like a heavy load had been lifted and I have served Him now almost forty-two years.

In the last twenty-five years, we have seen many changes in our church. Friends and loved ones have given their hearts to Christ. Friends and loved ones have passed away and gone on to reap their rewards, which we all hope to attain in making heaven our home.

Many loved ones and the elders of the church are now gone. They were the ones who taught us how to be faithful and steadfast in our faith. Now the people in my generation are the elders. I wonder, sometimes, what we are passing down to the next generation that is coming up behind us. Are we showing them the faithfulness and all the other things it takes to stand strong when trouble, trials, and heartaches come?

We are so blessed to have our pastor. He is the most compassionate and caring man that I know. He is always doing something for the Lord.

He is not one to follow a program. When the Spirit starts to move, he will stand back and let Him flow. He is fortunate to have our "First Lady," Sharon, as his wife, to be by his side in everything that he does. The church would be lost without her. We love them both dearly.

In 1991, a "God-sent" revival broke out. It started on a Sunday night with people getting saved and went on for two weeks. The excitement was so great, you could hardly wait for the next night of revival to see who was going to be saved. People were coming together not only from Union Hill but also from all around. If you wanted a good seat, you had to get there early or sit in the back. I will never forget this revival.

My son and his girlfriend (now his wife) were saved during the first week. Then on Friday, January 18th, 1991, my husband got saved. By that time, I had been saved sixteen years. Sometimes I grew a little weary of going to church by myself, but God answered my prayer and saved him. It didn't happen at church. He got saved in his truck. God can save you anywhere you are if you will just call upon Him.

In 2001, we had another revival, where we saw many people saved. God has blessed our church abundantly and beyond our expectations.

The building of our new church in 1991 and moving into it in 1992 were monumental events in our lives. You see, we moved into it debt free. We had no mortgage! Only God could do that. I am so proud to be a member of God's family that attends Union Hill Church.

MY SALVATION

Ronnie Shriver

I would like to share a part of my testimony. I was saved January 18, 1991, in the revival at Union Hill Church. My wife went to church without me for sixteen years. Don't ever give up on your spouse if they aren't saved because our timing is not God's timing.

Betty, my wife, had prayer meetings at our house. My brother-in-law, Bob Purtee, and I thought that if they wanted the fire, we would give it to them. We got an armload of slabs and put them in the old wood stove. The room heated up real fast. They opened the windows and doors but kept the prayer meeting going. I think the devil might have been working in us that night.

I would like to thank Big John Wesley for never giving up on me. He was always talking to me about the Lord. In fact, the day I got saved, he gave me a good talking to. Since then he has already gone on to be with the Lord.

This same day, I went to Frank Rowe's house in West Union. I had never been there before. I felt compelled to go but did not understand why (The Lord had this all planned out). Frank had left work early and was looking out the window when I pulled in. I walked in, and he showed me pictures of him and his wife being baptized.

All I could remember about Frank was how he had fought at the clubs where I had played in a band many years before. I knew I had to get out of there, but he wouldn't let me close the truck door. He just kept talking about the Lord.

I finally left and got to the bottom of Jacktown Hill. I thought I was having a heart attack. Then I told the Lord, *If this is You, take my life and do what you can with it.* It was no big prayer, but He knew my heart was ready to accept Him. I felt like I was floating in the truck.

When Betty came home from work, I never told her anything but just asked her to call Pastor Phil and have him stop by on his way to church. Well she knew something had happened because I never would have said that. I would usually shy away from being around him. He stopped, and we went to the bedroom and prayed. I was saved! I have never been the same since He came into my life!

Since 1991, every Sunday morning at 8:15 a.m., Frank Rowe would call and check on me. He has truly been an inspiration to me. I pray that my story will touch hearts and that God will bless you.

Union Hill Homecoming Service 2013

MY MEMORIES OF GROWING UP AT UNION HILL CHURCH

Brian Fulton (PK)

I have a lot of fond memories of being a preacher's kid (PK) and growing up in the little, white church on the hill. I remember the all-day meeting the church would have with dinner served on the ground, which actually lasted all day. The men would get to church early on Sunday and empty the Sunday school rooms of their tables and wooden chairs. The ladies of the church would also be up early preparing their favorite dishes for the dinner that day. We would have church and then take a break at around lunchtime to try to find a shaded area outside to eat lunch. After lunch, the tables and chairs were put back inside the rooms and the music started upstairs.

A lot of people who use to attend Union Hill always came back to our church for homecoming. I think all of them would either testify or sing to the congregation in the afternoon. They were never in a big hurry to end the services. They seemed to last a long time, but you could sure feel the Holy Spirit when people sang.

Back then, we didn't have air-conditioning in the church but had central air. It consisted of the windows being opened and the church fans moving back and forth.

Before the expansion of the church, the piano was positioned down on the floor near the first pew. While my mother, Sharon Fulton, played the piano, I would sit with her on the bench. She didn't like it when I touched the keys on the piano while she was playing the hymns the congregation was singing. After pulling my hands down or smacking them a few times, she would tell me to go and sit in a pew and behave.

After a few minutes of clapping my hands and tapping my feet, I would go and sit with my grandpa, Bud Swayne. For some reason, I tended to mind better when I sat next to Pap. If I would get a little loud, he would gently squeeze my leg. It was his sign that let me know I needed to settle down. If I got really bad, I had to go and stand by the pastor, who just happened to be my dad.

Once I had to stand by my dad with my arm around his leg. I tried to hide behind the podium while he was preaching to the congregation. Usually, if I got tired at church, I could be found sleeping under the coatrack in the back of the church by the water fountain.

A few years went by, and the church made some upgrades. Air-conditioning and stained-glass windows were installed and twelve feet was added onto the back of the church, which extended the pulpit area and included two new Sunday school rooms in the basement. The back stairway leading to the basement was taken out. A picture of Jesus with outstretched arms, which Truby Abbott painted, was put up. A side door was also added as an emergency exit, due to the expansion of the church.

When I was young, I heard numerous messages about salvation, heaven, and hell. Hell became very real to me one night at Union Hill. Someone had been invited to minister on a Saturday night. The congregation had been informed it was going to be a film about the Rapture and hell. Because I was only seven or eight years old, the only people I could recall ever bringing in slides and a projection screen had been missionaries.

When the lights were turned out and the film was rolling, all I remember was seeing the devil surrounded with fire and hearing the loud screams from those who were in hell. It really had an effect on me. I had nightmares for weeks after that.

Needless to say, when they were invited back the next year, I wasn't looking forward to it. That time, I hid my face under my mom's arm and put my hands over my ears. I didn't want to hear or see the torments those people were going through. After more nightmares of hell that ensued, I realized, even at that age, I didn't want to go to that awful place.

During the summers, the church always held a week of Vacation Bible School (VBS). A group of young students from a Christian college would come and oversee the VBS. The members of the group were always energetic and seemed to enjoy teaching us songs and games. The kids learned a lot from the puppets, which were used when the college students told us Bible stories. We always made cool crafts to take home.

As I got a little older, I was allowed to sit in the back of the sanctuary with some of my cousins. Pap used to say, "The back of the church is reserved for sinners and lovers."

During the second or third congregational song, Joe and Norma Jean Swayne usually arrived with Aunt Verda (BoBo) Grooms. BoBo sat in the middle of the sanctuary near the aisle. As a kid, I didn't like to sit next to her. She always pinched my cheeks and pulled my toes to get them to crack. That hurt.

On the other hand, we liked to sit near Joe and Norma Jean because they always had candy. What kid doesn't like candy? Every weekend, we would wipe out their supply of Tic Tacs, gum, and Certs.

I liked to sit in the back because there, we could talk, laugh, and make fun of people when the Holy Spirit started to move. Some folks do peculiar things when the Holy Ghost starts moving. As kids, we could tell real quick when the Holy Spirit was moving.

Faye Thompson would get up and sing "Ain't No Grave Gonna Hold My Body Down" and would start to bounce up and down and tap her hand on the podium. Then Eunice Minton would get up and help Faye sing. At that point, we knew what song was going to be next, "Sit Down. I Can't Sit Down." The congregation would begin to erupt as the people stood and clapped their hands.

We weren't tall enough, so we stood up on the pews to see over the adults in front of us. We witnessed some people shouting, some dancing in the Spirit, and some even running inside the church.

One night when the Spirit was moving on people, Ted Wesley ran around the inside of the church and then out the back doors. Two minutes later, he ran back into the church. Boy, was that a service. Back then, that was the norm. We usually got out of church at nine-thirty or ten o'clock. People came to mind the Lord and be led by the Holy Spirit.

Back then, the Sunday school format was a little different than what we are accustomed to today. Earnel Ward was the superintendent of the church. After singing some congregational songs, he would get up and read a scripture or a passage out of the Bible and then expound on what he had read. If no one needed prayer, we would be dismissed to our classes in the basement.

My first teachers were Bessie Ward and Norma Jean Swayne. Being so young, I don't remember much about the class other than the fact that we colored a lot of pictures pertaining to the Bible lesson that day.

My next teachers were Stella Mae Ward and Eunice Minton. We used to sit at a very short table, which is still used in our church today. Aunt Eunie, as I called her, taught us the Bible stories of baby Moses and David and Goliath with Bible characters she would stick on a felt board. What I remember most about Aunt Eunie was that her hairdo was always the same and she usually gave us animal crackers to snack on during class.

Next, I moved to a class where the teacher was young and had long red hair. Her name was Judy Ann Ward, and boy, did I like her class. She made the Bible lesson very interesting and was able to keep our attention. What I enjoyed most about her class was doing sword drills after our lesson was done. Judy Ann would call out a Bible verse, and all the kids would try to be the first one to find it. This activity really helped me learn where the books of the Bible were located.

Next, I was promoted to Toby Smalley's class, and boy, did we give him a run for his money. I can't count the times he threatened to take us to the pastor if we didn't stop talking and listen to the lesson. I looked at it as keeping Toby close to God because I'm sure he prayed a lot for us during our time in his class.

Randy Hamilton and his family started attending the church and after sometime, became my next teacher. By this time, I was into my early teenage years. Like most teenagers, I thought I was cool and didn't want to listen or participate.

I honestly think my next teacher, Judy Kay VanHoy, had been praying for patience when Jason Shriver and I arrived in her class. The Lord heard her prayer.

Looking back, we were pretty ornery. Jason and I were responsible for taking the offering and attendance up to Joe Swayne, the Sunday school treasurer. Jason had to remember the attendance. My job was to remember the amount of money in the offering. I usually forgot by the time we made it upstairs and would have to count it again. After getting a drink from the water fountain, making a trip to the bathroom, and then taking a second and third drink from the water fountain, we made our way back to class about ten minutes later.

By this time, Judy had already started teaching the lesson. Can you believe she wanted the teenagers in the class to take turns reading—out loud? Judy liked us to participate in class. She got us to do this by having us read and asking us questions. I wasn't a very fast reader but read when called upon. However, Judy probably regretted calling on Jason. When Jason read, he read everything on the page, and when I say everything, I mean everything. He read from the beginning of the sentence, through the punctuation in the middle, to the period at the end. We always chuckled when he read, and it never seemed to get old. I tried to duplicate it a few times, but it wasn't the same.

We could tell when we had pushed Judy's buttons too hard and would settle down. If Judy told us she had a headache that was her way of asking us to behave.

There were two doors to our classroom—the main one and a side door from the adjacent classroom. One day, we found a spool of yarn in the supply room and tied the main door's knob to the side door's knob. It was wrapped around so many times she couldn't open the main door to get into the room. She tried the other door but got the same result—the door wouldn't open. We had successfully locked our teacher out of the room. After a few minutes and a couple threats to get the Pastor, we cut the yarn to allow the door to open. Needless to say, after that, Judy always told us she had a headache.

I know it didn't seem like it, but we all had respect for Judy Kay. She knew we weren't serving the Lord but she always witnessed to us and told us about God. We all knew Judy prayed for us. We trusted her enough that we could go to her with any problem and know she would pray for and with us.

As I look back at all the great teachers I had in Sunday school, I know I was really blessed. Those ladies and men instilled the love of God in my life as well as in the other kids.

Around the age of thirteen or fourteen, Dad said he would buy me a set of drums if I would start playing them in church. I was playing drums in my school's band, so I said, "Sure! I can give it a try." After the twelve-foot addition was added onto the old church, the piano was moved to the platform and the drums were set up beside it. Because I was very shy, I hid behind the drums and played them softly until I became more comfortable playing in front of the church.

When Faye Thompson sang, she got offbeat and made it more challenging for me to keep up with her. However, I loved watching Bob Minton. No matter what the tempo of the song was, Bob strummed his guitar to the same slow steady beat. He usually had his eyes closed, but once in a while, I would see a tear run down his face. I knew right then, Bob was getting blessed.

Our church always welcomed testimonies. Usually, eight to ten people testified in each service. Some testimonies stood out to me more than others did. Johnny Ward would stand and say how much he loved the Lord. With tears running down his face, he would ask the congregation to pray for his boys to get saved.

Another person I remember was Sister May Duke. Sister May would get up and in a calm, mild voice, would talk about the good things of God. A little bit into her testimony, we all knew what was coming. Her voice started to get a little louder and before you knew it, it would begin to sound like a big train whistle: "Wheeeww," "Wheeeww,""Whew, Whew, Whew."

Some of the best services I ever witnessed at Union Hill happened during our foot washing services. As kids, we would help carry the hot water we would use to wash each other's feet, up from the basement to the front of the church. They would turn the front pews around on each side of the church so that they faced the second pews. Men would gather on one end and the women on the other. We would sit as close as we could and watch the Holy Spirit move. It's hard to explain these services, you just had to be there and experience them to understand. Several people would shout all over the church at different times.

After the revival in 1991, the young people who used to watch the foot washing had gotten saved. I remember washing other people's feet and what a humbling experience it was. When it was time for my feet to be washed, all I remember is closing my eyes, praying, and allowing the Holy Ghost to take over. It's better felt than told.

After being saved, I remember the services when the Holy Spirit would begin to move and those who were obedient would sometimes march around the altar or shout. Lisa Swayne (Brown), Beth Ann Fulton (Aber), Wendy Van Hoy (Purdin), Jeff Swayne, Jason Shriver, and others including myself are some of those who went from sitting in the back of the church to getting saved and moving toward the front.

At times, there was a full line of people marching around the altar. If you weren't in the line, someone might pull you out of your seat to take a lap or two with the people in line. I used to think church was boring when I sat in the back. After I gave my heart to God, I didn't realize how much better it was going to be at church until I participated in the worship and listened to the preaching.

Some people think that being a preacher's kid must have been hard. I mean, I can't count how many church services I've been in over the course of my life. I was there on Saturday night, Sunday morning, and Sunday night, as well as for the many revivals at Union Hill and other churches from Dayton to West Virginia. One thing's for sure, I wouldn't trade how I was raised for anything. I am honored to have had a great grandmother, Nora "Granny" Swayne, and a grandfather, Bud Swayne, who were original members of the Union Hill Church and faithfully served God with all their hearts. What a legacy and heritage I've been given. I've been very blessed.

October 2004 Faith and Freedom Tour
Judge Roy Moore, Pastor Fulton, and local pastors
Ten Commandments from Alabama court room

OH, THE MEMORIES!

JEFF SWAYNE

Though I am no longer a member of Union Hill Church, I try to come back as much as I can. I have always regarded it as my home church, which will take me from the cradle to the grave or to the return of our Lord. Some of my youngest memories were at Union Hill Church: Christmas plays, VBS, Mt. Hope Bible Camp, Sunday school, revivals, and prayer meetings. The family, friends, and relationships that formed have molded me into the person I am today.

When I think of Union Hill Church, the word that comes to mind is *faithfulness*. Sometimes dogmatic but undeniable is the faithfulness that Union Hill Church has shown to the surrounding communities and the people in those areas.

Since most of my life has been connected in one way or another to the church, finding specific times, memories, or stories to share was somewhat difficult to isolate. Some do come to mind, such as the time a few of us boys had a snowball fight in the basement of the old church while the service took place. While the preacher was speaking about hell, fire, and brimstone, we boys were trying to quench it with snowballs! We might have succeeded had the pastor not come down the steps and almost been hit by one! (I don't really remember who threw that one.)

If the adults had known the things that had happened, from time to time, in the back seats, well, let's just say I would have blistered my son's bottom! However, I do remember that whenever the Holy Spirit began to move, no matter where we were, every tongue became silent, every head was turned, and every heart was touched, giving its attention to the Spirit.

I remember the old guard: Harley Swayne, Ernald Ward, Troy Smith, Roby Perdue, and Bob Minton, just to name a few. I also remember the changing of that guard and the one who spanned that change, Pastor Phil Fulton. I remember my Sunday school teachers over the years: Eunice Minton, Sharon Fulton, Toby Smalley, Judy Ward, Judy VanHoy, and Brenda Spriggs.

They all had an impact on my life, especially Toby. In my opinion, he went above and beyond the call, to reach out to us youths in the church. I remember all the outings with Brian, Jason, Joe, and Shane. I can only hope and pray that somewhere, at some time, someone will reach out to my children the same way they did to make a difference in their lives.

Probably one of the greatest memories I have of the church was the revival of 1991. I remember Ruby (Big Mom) coming in every night and saying, "Do you want me to tell you who got saved tonight?" Well after about three weeks of this, I remember saying, "No, I don't!" I was under conviction but was just too stubborn to give in at that time. What no one knows is that I would drive up to the church during the revival, stop, and listen, many times.

I remember the night I gave in to the invites and came to 1991 revival. Toby came and asked me to pray with him. I was under so much conviction, my nose started bleeding, but still I held out. I don't know why I did this. I guess I was just stubborn and bullheaded.

I held out until Easter of 1991. I remember coming into the church, sitting in the back pew, and starting to shake as soon as the service began. When the altar call was given, I practically ran over to Ottie Hilterbrand, who always stood next to the aisle on the left side of the old church (facing the pulpit).

I read a poem when I was a freshman in high school by Robert Frost called "The Road Not Taken." The end of the poem says, "Two roads diverged in a wood, and I—I took the one less traveled by, and that has made all the difference." That Easter Sunday in 1991, I made the choice of taking a less beaten path. The path has had its ups and downs, has been rough and smooth, and has been hard and easy at times. However, I praise God that he led me to the beginning of this path at Union Hill Church. I shall never forget my beginnings and the people I met there.

May God bless you in this worthy endeavor, which you have undertaken, to create a history book of our church. I enjoyed reminiscing on the memories of my birth (spiritually). I appreciate what you have done and what you are doing.

Judy Kay VanHoy

THE SPAN OF YEARS

Judy Kay VanHoy

Union Hill Church has always been my home church. Back when I was a child at Union Hill, the people at Mt. Zion and Burns Chapel would go to each other services. We went to Union Hill for Saturday night services, Burns Chapel for Sunday School, and Mt. Zion for Sunday night services, but it was all the same people. We just chose one as our home church and that was Union Hill.

Mom and us kids had been raised a half mile down the road from Union Hill Church. Mom would often tell us how she, her mom, and her grandma would walk to church and the power of God would fall and bless them.

Mom was saved at the age of sixteen. Dad wasn't saved until later in life but many times, would testify, saying, "In 1963, the Spirit of the Lord came on Forest Thompson and I, and we rolled on the floor right over there," which was between the altar and the pew.

Union Hill has been and still is a church with praying people, who believe the Lord can save, heal, and deliver what they need. Mom had a wooden chair, which sat by the kitchen door where everyone walked by it to come in the house. At night, she never went to bed until she had knelt at that chair and prayed and prayed. Dad did his praying in the barn. No wonder they prayed so much. The good Lord had blessed them with ten children.

For as long as I can remember, I loved going to church. When folks prayed, the power came down, and we kids in the back seats gave all of our attention to what was happening in the front.

Joyce, my younger sister, was only nine years old when she got saved.

She served the Lord for the rest of her life. She led the congregational singing and was a Sunday school teacher and a janitor. Eunice Minton taught her how to play the guitar and the piano. She was young but sure had a love for the Lord and was willing to do anything for Him. She carried a burden for me.

I finally gave my heart to the Lord in 1974 after I became a wife and mother. Union Hill was having a revival. Joyce sent me a letter telling me about the revival and how God had told her to write to me. She said the letter was wet with her tears. This broke my heart, so on Saturday night with my little girls in tow, I went to church.

We had just sat down when Joyce sang a song that was especially for me. I went to the altar and prayed a long time that night. Even though I got slain in the Spirit, I just didn't feel like I was saved. I came back Sunday morning, and God gloriously saved me. I began to help Mom and Norma Jean Swayne with Sunday school or to do anything that they needed me to do.

Two years after I was saved, the Lord called me to preach. This wasn't easy for me to accept. I tried to run but got so miserable I had to say, "Yes." I led the service and ended up preaching a little, thinking nobody knew I had been called to preach but me. I would pray, *Lord, please don't let anyone know.* Bud Swayne was the first elder and was supposed to lead the service but would ask me to do it. So I couldn't hide very well from the anointing.

One night when I couldn't take it anymore, I asked my pastor to go with me downstairs and told him what was going on. He just smiled while I cried so hard I was shaking. God had already told him. I asked him, "Why didn't you tell me?" He said, "Because you had to accept it."

At that time, there were few if any women preachers. In my carnal mind, I thought God wouldn't receive me. Oh boy, the devil was a liar. The Lord had prepared the way. I have served as a Sunday school teacher, preacher, youth leader, ladies' ministry leader, Warriors Prayer Meeting leader, missionary leader, evangelist and have assisted with Bible school.

My first message was Matthew 10:26–31 and was titled "Fear." I sure knew what that was. The North family sang that night, and the church was packed. Some came just to hear a woman preacher, but when I began, the anointing came and everything was okay. When God calls us, if we do our parts, then He will do His.

I have so many memories. I've taught just about every class except the adult class. It seemed like the teen and young adult class was where I belonged. The Lord would wake me up at night and tell me what some of those kids had done on Saturday night. One of my classes was so lost, but we had a revival, and just about all of them got saved. We talk a lot about Brian Fulton and Jason Shriver being ornery boys, and they were, but there were so many more. I figure I had better not mention them. Though they were ornery, I could tell the difference when they respected me and when they didn't.

God would always dust me off, and I would go back for more. Ryan Lewis told me he cried all the way home the Sunday I told him I needed a break and wouldn't be his teacher any longer. He thought that because he and Tyler Ward had been so ornery, they had caused me to stop teaching (Sometimes we just need a break).

Billy Purtee would hide under my desk so Tim, who was the Sunday school superintendent, wouldn't see him and make him go to another class. Of course, I wanted to keep my kids. I've been and still am blessed to be able to teach such great kids. Now I'm teaching the kids whose parents were in my class a few years ago.

When I was the youth leader, we did so many fun things, such as a hayride each fall. Brenda Spriggs would help me, and we would play games, roast hot dogs, and take a long ride on the hay wagon pulled by a tractor. Ronnie Anderson was usually the driver. We would have Christmas for the kids, make crafts, read Bible stories, and of course, pray. We participated in sword drills at West Union. The kids would study really hard. They brought home trophies, ribbons, and even the Bible sword.

To help inspire unity in the youth group and just to have fun, I would take them on trips to Tennessee and once, to Florida. The kids had to work in order to go on the trips. One of their jobs was cleaning yards for people.

One time when we were cleaning a yard, there was a pile of wood by the porch. One of the kids picked up the wood to find many, and I mean many, snakes! J. C. Lowe, who was one of my boys, grabbed me and pulled me away from them because he knew I was terrified of snakes.

We washed people's windows and the outsides of their houses. We asked for donations. We all worked hard to earn our way. It was worth it all to get to be with the kids. Of course, when we did the car washes or anything that had to do with water, everyone got wet.

On one trip to Tennessee, Julie Purtee and Gina Smalley wanted to bungee jump. I told them no, but before we came home, guess what? Gina and Julie bungee-jumped. I thought, *Their parents will sue me*, but God was good again. They lived through it and so did I.

We never went to bed on these trips until we had gathered for devotions and prayer. One night, we had a house for the boys and one for the girls. Walt was with the boys. They woke him up in the middle of the night and told him they heard a bear outside. So out they all went but only found a raccoon having supper.

One of the most vital parts of my youth ministry was the youth prayer meetings that we held. The Holy Ghost spoke to us and gave us encouragement, warnings, and revelations about our lives. Oh, it was so good!

Pastor Phil wanted us to come upstairs when the main service started. During one of those meetings, the kids were filled with the Holy Ghost. The Spirit was really moving. Kids lay on the floor by the Spirit and spoke in tongues—that beautiful, heavenly language. When we finally made it upstairs, we went down the church aisle shouting and praising the Lord. The service broke, and everyone was shouting.

Once we had an all-night prayer meeting at Dave and Lisa Brown's house. The kids prayed, and the glory of God came down. My, those teens sure knew how to pray. Gina Smalley interceded for hours. Michelle Roland and Jason Shriver shouted. Their house had a closet in the middle so you could walk around the house in a circle. That night we all went around and around praising the Lord. You talk about a Spirit-filled meeting! That was one! The Lord has been so good to me!

Ladies' prayer meetings were so special. We saw so many results.

Louise Hilterbran had cancer on her face. We anointed her that morning. That evening she would be going to an appointment to have it removed. When she went home from the prayer meeting, it dropped off.

We prayed for people to be saved, and when we came to church on the weekend, they got saved. A lot of wrecks kept happening, and people we knew were getting killed. We prayed that the wrecks would stop, and they did. Folks would come needing to hear from the Lord, and God would give them a word of encouragement.

For thirty-eight years, we had the ladies' prayer meeting. We made Thanksgiving dinner for our widows and widowers. We each would make something. We brought enough to feed all of them. We filled their plates so full, they were able to make two meals out of it. In the beginning, we would meet at Ruby and Bud's house. She would always make noodles. Oh, my! They were so good! Then we would map out a route and take it to them. We would also have Christmas dinners and a mother daughter banquet each year. We did so many things for the Lord.

Our missionary ministry was very rewarding work. We supported many missionaries in our own neighborhoods and abroad. We helped send these young people to the mission field and assisted the locals in building schools and hospitals. A missionary in Africa needed a car. Bev Bick, Marvin Bick, Walt VanHoy, and many more got together and held fund-raisers, yard sales, and plant sales so that we could buy this missionary a car. God supplied the money, and he now has a car that we try to keep tires on. To God be the glory!

Gina Smalley and Julie Purtee at Barboursville

Gina Smalley, Kim Browning, Julie Purtee, and
Wendy VanHoy on youth trip to Tennessee

Youth trip to Tennessee

Ladies' retreat in Barbourville, Kentucky

Kathy Finlaw

LIVING IN THE REALM OF HIS PEACE

December 14, 2003

Katheryn L. Finlaw

There have been many times I've felt God and His peace—
In moments of laughter, sorrow, and even danger.
Many times, through this peace came tears of joy as the Spirit moved.
At times, there came boldness as I was to be obedient.
So many times, through so many things, I have experienced the peace
    of God.
But, oh my, what a spiritual high it is to live within the realm of His
    peace,
When you get to a point where self-will totally leaves your heart,
And God begins to move and start a work within you—
Not just for a moment or a day but totally and completely.
It almost feels like you live in a different dimension at times.
There is this amazing peace, and you feel no worry.
You can feel the things that are going on around you and within you.
Things that would normally upset you don't seem to affect you.
It's like you just know God has everything in control.
Your body goes through the motions,
But your spirit is in the realm of His peace.
As you look in the eyes of the people around you,
You see their pain as they look at you.
I realized my body was very sick and many things did it endure.
I was often asked if I was scared, and I simply answered no.

I would ask the Lord, at times, to let me sleep continually.

I would start to pray for others and the sleep would come.

The fear had set in on those around me as they watched my body weaken.

Still there was no fear in me. I was in the realm of His peace.

The saints of God must have overladen heaven with prayers just for me,

And those cherished prayers, every one of them, touched my heart.

Hands were laid upon me; cries rang out for my healing.

They went up like sweet savors unto the Lord.

Daily my health improves in a supernatural way.

As the Lord does His work, both physically and spiritually.

Like the scriptures say, words cannot describe the fullness of God's grace.

This, my friend, is my version of living in the realm of His peace.

GOD HAS HEALED MY CANCER OF THE TONGUE!

Kathy Finlaw

In May of 2002, I was invited to a Union Hill Church ladies' retreat. I was so impressed with the love that the women showed me. I started attending the church. At that time in my life, I had backslidden on the Lord. During the services that weekend, the Lord spoke to me, deep within my soul. I have been part of the church ever since.

In July 2003, I was diagnosed with Stage IV tongue cancer. Among the many things the doctors said to me were, "We will have to remove your tongue," and, "We only give you six months to live." My response to the doctor was, "God's got this." I knew that the Lord would choose to either heal me here on earth or take me home to heaven for my ultimate healing. My mind didn't war against my body. Hence, I wrote the poem, "Living in the Realm of His Peace."

As the side effects came from the treatments, so did the love and compassion from my church family. Pastor Phil and Sister Sharon showed up at my house late one Friday night to pray for me. Judy Kay VanHoy rallied twenty prayer warrior ladies, who were willing to do a twenty-one-day Daniel fast for my healing. This was the first Daniel fast the church had ever done. I received many cards. Because I wasn't able to work, the church helped me with my finances.

I was hospitalized a few times. One of those times, my mother was hospitalized also. I was in Hillsboro, and she was in Cincinnati. She had to undergo open-heart surgery. Pastor Phil and Sister Sharon went to be with my family during my mother's surgery. They then drove straight to the hospital where I was to let me know how she was doing.

I went for six weeks without being able to eat a bite of food. Water was the only thing that I could halfway tolerate. To the eyes of most people around me, I was losing the battle. My church family never let up in their prayers and never gave up on me. I had become so weak I wasn't able to walk and was barely functioning.

My dad pleaded to take me to church. He had to bring me in with a wheelchair. The church laid hands on me that night and began to pray. Wow! The Holy Ghost's power came down. The next morning, I was hungry. I was only able to eat one little slice of orange, but it was the start of being able to eat again.

In my doctors transcripts he had written, "Things are worsening. We will probably have to dissect her neck." When I returned the following Monday, his notes said, "She never ceases to amaze me. She said her church prayed for her."

It is now July 2016 and I still have my tongue. There is not a trace of cancer in my body. My God is real and faithful, and so is my Union Hill Church family. To God be the glory!

October 4, 1997, Promise Keepers trip to Washington DC

September 2001, Old Timers Day Parade, first place for most religious

Trip to the Creation Museum

Phil and Tessa Swayne Family

TRIBUTE TO PHIL SWAYNE

Tessa Swayne

Phillip Lee Swayne and Tessa (Taylor) Swayne

Phillip: First Elder, Choir Director, Praise and Worship Leader

Tessa: Elementary Youth Leader

If you knew Phillip, you knew he was a humble and wise man. Phillip was also a quiet man, who took time to think before he spoke and to read every single detail in the instruction manual before he put anything together. This is how he lived his life.

Phillip Lee Swayne was the son of Harley and Ruby Swayne. He was born June 22, 1959. While growing up on the farm, he helped his father and attended church every week.

Phillip developed a love for music at a very young age. Tessa remembers him telling her about the time he got a transistor radio and how he would hide under the covers at night to listen to the Grand Ole Opry on WSM. He taught himself how to play the guitar with a little help from his uncle Jim Grooms.

After graduating high school, Phillip attended Ohio State University and graduated with a bachelor of science in agricultural education. Once he completed his student teaching, he decided that teaching was not what he wanted to do for the rest of his life.

While he attended Ohio State, he worked at the campus's radio station and enjoyed this very much. He worked at various stations, with the last one being C103.1 WRAC in West Union, Ohio, as the general manager. He worked at this station for eight years.

Phil began evaluating his life. He decided that if he stayed at the radio station he could not afford a family with the salary he was making. He made a pact with himself that if he had not found that special person by the time he turned thirty, he would be satisfied with what he was doing.

However, he met that special person in January of 1989, and the search for a new career began. He was accepted into the training program for the Farm Service Agency, a branch of the USDA. He would finally use his degree. He accepted a position as the office manager in the Pike County FSA office. This paved the way for the marriage of Phillip to Tessa Taylor on June 2, 1990.

Phillip began to evaluate his life again. He knew something was missing. Phillip was raised knowing his rich Christian heritage. He knew the importance of raising a family with godly values. He and Tessa started to attend the services at Union Hill Church with Phillip's parents and several other family members.

On December 28, 1991, Union Hill Church was in a revival, and the minister was Mark Baer. At this service, the Holy Spirit tugged at both Phillip's and Tessa's heart. Eunice Minton asked them if they wanted to pray, so together they began their journey. They were baptized in May of 1992, by Pastor Phil Fulton and Reverend Boyd Young.

With a new life and a journey, Phillip began playing and singing at weekly services while Tessa became a Sunday school teacher. As they worked for the Lord, they also participated in the choir and prayer meetings. They had great mentors in the church to teach them what it meant to serve the Lord and to be faithful.

Tessa began to help with the teen group while Phillip continued to focus on the music in the church. The group Set Free was formed at this time, and it included Phillip, Bobby Minton, and Ronnie Shriver. Together they had a sweet harmony, which would welcome the sweet Holy Spirit every time they sang. Many local churches invited them to sing at their revivals. They traveled around until they were needed more at Union Hill.

With his love and passion for music and the anointing of the Holy Spirit, Phillip worked diligently on the music for the church. With the rich heritage he grew up in, he knew that he needed to be committed to the Lord 100 percent and not just halfway. He strived to give his very best to the Lord. He would spend hours in prayer and working on the music.

On January 30, 1993, Phillip and Tessa welcomed a new, bouncing, baby boy, Zachary Taylor Swayne, into their family. On November 21, 1994, they welcomed a beautiful, blue-eyed, little girl, Emilee Melissa Swayne. With their family complete, they continued giving to the Lord and raising their children to know who Jesus was.

Because Phillip was very talented, he was frequently asked to lead the praise and worship at the beginning of the service as well as to finish up with the altar call song at the end of each service. Phillip also keyed all the music for the musicians, especially for his sister, Sharon Fulton, who played the piano.

It didn't take long before Phillip was leading the choir. In January 2008, the church board approached him to ask if he would accept the position of first elder. He graciously accepted. This allowed Phillip to continue his passion for music and to follow God's call.

Phillip always sought the guidance of the Holy Spirit and felt very uneasy if he did not get the direction from God on how the service should go. Tessa continually told him, "Calm down. God will give you direction when the time is right."

Phillip and Tessa continued to work in the church. His focus was on the music. Her focus was on the youth. In 2001, she started the new elementary program on Wednesday nights for the kids. Faithfulness, commitment, and willingness to be used by God were the traits the elders taught, and they learned to follow them.

In 2014, a new singing group was created with a couple of dear gentlemen, Chester Hatfield and Tom Bosier, which Phillip came to love. This group was known as the Bluegrass Boys. Phillip enjoyed having them over for practice sessions. They introduced him to the banjo and the mandolin. It was a delight to hear them play songs like "I'll Fly Away," "A House of Gold," and "Hold to God's Unchanging Hand."

In late February of 2015, Phillip was diagnosed with esophageal cancer Stage IV. He underwent several chemo treatments. With each treatment the cancer shrank. His prayer was that God would give him strength for this new journey and would continue to use him in the music ministry. He prayed that he would continue to have a good appetite, as he loved Tessa's cooking. He also prayed he would not lose his hair, as he loved it as well. God honored his prayers.

God's anointing was very strong in Phillip's life. He put his whole heart into the songs that he sang for the Lord. One of the highlights at this time in Phillip's life was when the gospel group, The Bowling Family, came to Union Hill Church. They invited Phillip to join them while they sang. This was such an honor and a blessing to him.

Phillip completed his journey on earth on September 6, 2015, and won the crown of glory and eternal life with Jesus Christ. This quiet and humble man gained his wisdom and knowledge by reading and studying the Word of God. To this day, if you open his Bible, you will see the many verses throughout it, which are circled or underlined. These verses explain very simply how Phillip lived his life.

Phillip's Favorite Bible Verses

The steps of a good man are ordered by the Lord, and He delights in his ways. (Ps. 37:23 KJV)

Enter into His gates with thanksgiving, and into His courts with praise. Be thankful to Him, and bless His name. (Ps. 100:4 KJV)

The fear of the Lord is the beginning of wisdom; a good understanding have all those who do His commandments. His praise endures forever. (Ps. 111:10 KJV)

Therefore whoever humbles himself as this little child is the greatest in the kingdom of heaven. (Matt. 18:4 KJV)

Phillip Lee Swayne was a humble man of integrity, knowledge, and wisdom. Above all, he loved all those around him.

Sunday school picnic at Fort Hill

Larry Joe Swayne, Tonya Rae Swayne, Stacy Johnson,
Billy Joe Swayne, Hunter Johnson, and Colt Johnson

SUNDAY SCHOOL AT UNION HILL CHURCH

TONYA SWAYNE

Ever since I started attending Union Hill Church, Sunday school has been an integral part of the church. We believe that it is vital for the well-being of our youth and adults that we teach them the Word of God. The Sunday school, which has classes for people from preschool all the way up to adults, has a superintendent, secretary-treasurer, and teachers.

I have been the Union Hill Sunday school treasurer since August 17, 1997, to the present. Before this, my father-in-law, Joe Swayne, was the Sunday school treasurer. He had some health issues so I assisted him with his duties. Come 2017, I will have been the Sunday school treasurer for twenty years. Joe Swayne retired from being the treasurer in August of 1997. At our annual Christmas dinner in 1997, he was presented with a plaque and a lift chair for his many years of service.

Earnel Ward was the Sunday school superintendent when we moved into the new church and held that position until Tim Howe took it over. Jeff Swayne and Ronnie Anderson were Tim's assistant superintendents, though not at the same time. After Tim Howe resigned, Lisa Howe took it over until Lisa Brown and Jeff Cutler became co-superintendents, which they still are at this time.

Each year the Sunday school provides money for the following: Mother's Day gifts, Father's Day gifts, Bible school, Easter treats, Christmas treats, Mt. Hope Bible Camp, high school graduates' gifts, van ministry, and the Christmas sharing program. It also presents Christmas gifts every year to all of our teachers, assistants, superintendents, treasurers, and van drivers in appreciation of their service and as a way to say thank you. For several years, we also had teacher's conferences to help them in their endeavors as they taught the children about God.

Each year, we collected money for our Christmas sharing program. This actually began as a home missions project under the missionary program at Christmas in 1996. Originally, the missionary president, Toby Smalley, listened to several complaints about having to fill out Christmas cards for all church members, especially since they saw them each weekend. He felt that instead of spending money on the cards, we could take that same money and use it to help families in need.

The church loved the idea. The money they would have spent on cards for church members was donated and used to help families in need. Later this was put under the Sunday school program. Money was donated during the month of November, and at Christmas, we helped as many families, who needed our help, as we could.

We have also supported the Gideons, the Jordan Ministry, Mt. Hope Bible Camp, and our missionary, Arlene Miller, in the past. Our average yearly expense runs eight thousand dollars and up. Our average yearly income runs around seven thousand and eight hundred dollars and up. We have even entered several Old Timers Day parades.

Sunday school put on an annual picnic the third Sunday of July for many years. I think it was started by Joe Swayne and Virgil Ballard and was always held at Fort Hill. The picnic moved to GE Employee Park when Tim Howe was the superintendent. In 2011, the date changed to the Sunday after Labor Day to help avoid the heat and was moved to Longs Retreat, which has been a great success. The Sunday school provides all meat, drinks, bread/buns, and supplies for this annual event.

The largest crowd to attend Sunday school, outside of our new church dedication, was at our Easter service in 1998. There were 237 people present. When our community center was built in 2000, my husband, Larry Swayne, and his company did all the HVAC work. The building was heated and cooled by heat pumps. The Sunday school also bought the athletic equipment for the center.

Larry, who grew up in the church, did all the HVAC and plumbing work in the new church also. He donated all the labor and equipment. The material was at cost. He removed one unit from the old church, and it is still working in our new church. It had two air handlers in the attic and three furnaces with air-conditioning.

In the old church, I was the janitor from July 1978 to July 1980 and the nursery teacher from 1984 to 1991. I continued to be the nursery teacher in the new church until 1994. This class consisted of children who were walking age thru kindergarten. This was a very large class. We had plenty of room in the new church, so when I left the class, it was divided between nursery and preschool aged children.

Teaching this class was a blessing as I saw the children learn and ask questions. I had many children come and go from my class. As teachers, we pray that students will retain something in their little minds, which they can take with them and will remember forever.

The church's small children use to have a penny march each Sunday morning. They would go up to the front of the church on Sunday morning to sing. They also brought their pennies and dropped them in a large jar. They thought this was great. Everyone would dig all his or her pennies out and hand them to the kids as they were going up front so that no child was without pennies. We had our last jar in 1999. These pennies would be counted when the jar was full and put into the treasury. Eunice Minton was the leader of these little children for many years.

We used to put on a Bible school where the members would teach, give snacks, and pick up children every day for a week for Bible school. We also had missionary groups that came in and taught the children. Then we moved it to Sundays for four or five weeks.

My full name is Tonya Rae Smalley Swayne. I became associated with the church in 1969 when I was a freshman in high school. Robin Swayne wanted me to go out on a date with her cousin Larry Joe. I asked my mom, and she said yes, as long as it was a double date. Some Saturday and Sunday nights, he took me to church. This was back when it seemed that everybody was related in some way or another. We continued to date for four years and married on June 23, 1973, in the old church, eight days after I had turned eighteen and had graduated from high school.

I gave my heart to the Lord on February 18, 1977, at a revival Larry's grandpa, Reverend Autumn Scott was holding at Beechfork Church. I was baptized in the creek along with Tammy Ballard Atkins and Pam Ward on Sept 25, 1977.

My husband, Larry Swayne, has been coming to Union Hill Church since he was five years old, when his family moved from Sidney, Ohio, back to the Locust Grove area and purchased a farm on Conaway Road in Smokey Corner. He remembers the old potbellied stove they had in the middle of the floor to keep warm and the outhouses they used for restrooms.

Larry was saved on April 28, 1979, during a revival while Gary Brown was preaching at our church. He was baptized in the creek on July 22, 1979. He was baptized by his uncle, Russell Lee Scott, who was a minister. Exactly one year later, our son Billy Joe was born on July 22, 1980. We also have a daughter, Stacy Michele, who was born on December 1, 1975, the day of his mother's birthday.

My maiden name is Smalley, and as I stated before, we were married in the old church on June 23, 1973. Union Hill is the church our family still attends today. Two grandsons were born to our daughter and her husband Randall Johnson. Our grandson Hunter is thirteen years old, and his brother, Colt, is nine years old. They also attend the church.

I would not trade my journey of serving the Lord for anything. I will strive even harder so I will be able to see all my loved ones who are already there.

Missionary work

THE 1997 FLOOD CLOTHING DRIVE MINISTRY

Christine Brabson

In 1997, God moved on a group of members at Union Hill Church. The Lord had laid on their hearts that they should begin a clothing drive. Little did they know that God was preparing the church to minister in all the local counties in our area of southern Ohio.

There were too many people involved in this ministry to name names, but a committee was formed, and the clothing drive was organized. People began to bring in so much clothing that the church's basement was packed. People also donated a lot of time to this ministry. One that I will name is Alton Swayne. He did most of the deliveries to those in need. He was a vital spoke in the wheel that was turning in this ministry.

Then the 1997 flood hit Adams County as well as other counties along the Ohio River and in their low-lying areas. Many homes and churches were damaged and some even washed away. God had prepared our little church body. We helped every family that needed clothing and nonperishable items.

During this time, an anonymous person, who did not go to church, donated a check. It was for approximately ten thousand dollars. God made it possible for us to help many people with their material needs. We even donated to another local church, which had been destroyed in the flood, and helped it rebuild.

We here at Union Hill thank the Lord for preparing us to minister to the material needs of those who were affected by the flood but thank

Him even more that we were able to touch them spiritually also. The members of Union Hill were listening to God when He spoke, and because they listened, they were ready to minister when the needs arose. To God be the glory!

1998 Old Timers Day youth singing

Youth church competition sword drills

The future church, Kaitlyn York, Megan Brown,
Isaac Brabson, Jessica Aber, and Blake Swayne

HOW GOD BROUGHT US TO UNION HILL CHURCH

Brother Stan and Sister Kay Helton

In early 1992, we knew the Lord was going to move us to another church. I told Stan I wasn't going anywhere until I heard from the Lord. With much prayer and waiting, the Lord showed us. In August 1992, we were both working. When I woke up one morning before my feet hit the floor, I heard in my spirit, *Go to Brother and Sister Howard's church.*

That evening, I was cooking, and Stan was talking. I thought, *When he is finished I will tell him what the Lord gave me this morning.* Then out of his mouth came, "The Lord said to go to Brother and Sister Howard's church." At that time, we did not know about Union Hill Church.

I called Sister Howard, and she gave me directions to the church. We came to a Saturday night service and loved it. Stan had been teaching an adult Sunday school class in our other church and had to tell them we were leaving.

Stan and Kay Helton

SAVED ON JUNE 10, 2012

Sunday Homecoming Service

Ronnie McIntosh

The following is a true story but the names are fictional.

Around September 2014, I was down at the Locust Grove Dairy Bar picking up my order when I saw one of the ladies from our church. We talked about when my wife, Jill, and I had gotten saved. The lady said she hadn't thought my wife was going to make it out of the church. She asked me if Jill had had cancer because she had looked so sick. I told her it had been from drinking alcohol and not eating.

Jill had gotten down to eighty-four pounds. She hadn't even known who I was when I had taken her to the hospital. The doctor had told me that she might die. It had taken Jill two days before she had known who I was.

After these events, the Lord kept dealing with me to give a testimony, but I didn't really want to go up to the pulpit in front of the church because I was scared to talk in front of people. My mother died that September. At her funeral, I got up and told the church about my mother and about how much I loved her. Then I read a verse out of the Bible from Revelation 21:4. Around one or two weeks went by and the Lord kept dealing with me to give my testimony, so I told our pastor what I wanted to do and am so glad I did.

In 2010, two years before we got saved, Jill wanted to go back to church. We had backslidden from the Lord in 1996. I didn't want to go because I did not want to give up my beer and drugs. Jill and I had started to drink every day and night and to take Percocet. We had begun to dive into a dark life that we could not control. Then beer and wine became 100 percent of our lives.

Jill went to rehab in Falmouth, Kentucky. I thought I could quit on my own but that never happened. Jill stayed in rehab four days and sober for two months. Then we both started drinking again. This time it got worse.

Around February of 2013, I became very depressed to the point that I didn't want to live anymore. One evening, I thought, *This is it. I will kill myself tonight.* We had friends over for a cookout, and as I was eating my dinner, I got up and told everybody I would be back in a few minutes. I went to the garage and found some rope. Then I got on my ATV, tied the rope to a rafter, and put the rope around my neck. Then I asked God to forgive me.

As I started to jump off my ATV to kill myself, I almost fell. Then it was like God spoke to me and said, "No." He held me back. So I thought, *Not now but maybe later.* Then weeks went by, and we went back to more drinking and depression. It was so bad. We just got worse and worse.

Jill wouldn't eat. All she did was drink, day and night. I came home from work one day, and she was drunk but didn't' know who I was. I called the doctor, and he said to bring her in. I took her to the hospital. The doctor said she was dying. If she could make it through the night, she might live.

She was at Good Samaritan, so I stayed with my mother. Mom was a good Christian. She and my sister got saved in the church that Jill and I had backslidden from. I remember Mom saying, "I am praying for Jill and you." Mom asked me to go to church with them when Jill was still in the hospital so I went that Wednesday night. I went to the altar to stand in for Jill. I felt good but was still drinking. Jill got out of the hospital after two weeks.

Her doctor wanted to put her in a nursing home for two to three months. He said that I couldn't take care of her. Jill was on her way to hell. She weighed eighty-four pounds. I had to give her showers, and she could barely walk. She had to use a walker.

At this time, she didn't drink. I was still drinking and taking pain pills. Then Jill said she wanted a glass of wine with her dinner. She began to drink again. The first night she got ahold of a bottle of wine and drank the whole thing. We both got worse. I was drinking about a case of beer a day. Then depression hit me hard.

I couldn't do anything. Jill and I were drunk all the time, and I didn't want to live anymore. One night, I was extremely depressed as I drank beer and wine. Jill had passed out on the couch. I was crying and went into the bedroom to get my shotgun. I told myself that this time I would kill myself but was going to shoot Jill first. I pointed the gun at Jill, but the gun didn't go off, so I fell on the floor, cried, and tried to drink myself to sleep.

About two weeks after that, the Lord started to deal with me. On June 8, four days before we got saved, I woke up feeling really depressed. I could hardly walk. I felt sick when I took a drink, so I told Jill I needed to go to the VA hospital. I told Jill I needed psychiatric help.

I went to the VA in Chillicothe, which was forty-three miles from our house, to talk to this psychiatrist. He said my problem was Jill and that I drank because she did. He gave me a prescription for panic attacks. He said not to drive when I took them. I didn't listen to him. Jill did not know I had taken them.

We left to go back home. When I was driving home, everything looked and felt funny. Then I felt like someone was telling me I needed to die. I couldn't see anything but the brake light from a car that was not there. I almost ran off the road. Then I ran someone off the road. Jill was telling me to stop the car. She was crying and wanted to know what was wrong with me.

She then started to drive. She drove about five or six miles and started having brake trouble. I told her I could drive, so I did but almost wrecked the car three times. It took us around three hours to get home.

Jill went to rehab on Thursday night in Ashland, Kentucky. She called me Friday morning and said she wanted to come home, so I went and got her Friday afternoon. We were still drinking. Then Jill and I decided we were going to church the next Sunday, no matter what.

We went to Union Hill three or four times before we got saved. The pastor and his son came to our house a couple of times. Out of all the churches we went to, the pastor at Union Hill was the only one who came to our house to visit us.

On June 10, 2012, we got saved! I thank Jesus for saving my life. Without Jesus we wouldn't be alive. Our lives belong to Him. Jesus took all of our sins on Himself and died so we could be *free*! I thank Jesus for saving our lives.

After we got saved, Jill and I were going to one of the other local churches. One day, we were having a yard sale at our house when a lady and her friend came and invited us to Union Hill Church. We hadn't been able to find a church that we felt comfortable in, so we went and tried it out. We felt like Union Hill Church was where God wanted us to go.

The Lord wanted us to go to Union Hill. I believe that. Our prayer is, "Lord save our people and don't let anyone live life the way we did before we got saved."

Baptism in the local creek

Toby and Joyce Smalley

WHAT AN HONOR

Toby and Joyce Smalley

It has been an honor and privilege for my wife Joyce and I to serve the Lord in various capacities throughout the years at Union Hill Church. I was saved at the church on February 12, 1981. I was under so much conviction that I ran all the way to Houston, Texas, to get away from God. I found out that God was also in Texas. Joyce got saved at Sciotoville Christian Baptist Church in June of 1981. We met in a revival service at White Oak Chapel and married at Union Hill on June 27, 1985.

In the 1980s, I began to teach in the old church. I took over the intermediate class for Sharon Day after she got married and moved away. I taught that class in the new church as well as the juniors. Later I taught the senior class.

I also became missionary leader in the 1980s and held that position in the new church until 1998, when I became the youth leader. I also oversaw the men's prayer meeting, which met each Monday night, and the single men's group, which met a few times a month.

Joyce was voted in as janitor while we were in the old church. She held that position in the new church until 1999. In 1992, she became the first choir director of the church and was in that position until 1999. God moved in the ministries that we were in. We counted it an honor and a privilege to be able to work for God and the church in these various positons.

In all the years that I have been saved, the church always had a choir but no choir director. In the old church, our pastor's wife, Sharon, played the piano and picked the songs, but in the new church, she and the pastor felt they needed an actual choir director. God had been moving on Joyce. She was a very good singer and had an anointing when she sang. The Lord had been dealing with her about taking the position, but she was reluctant to step out until Bud Brabson told her she needed to mind the Lord.

Later she spoke to the pastor, he agreed, and she became the first choir director. God moved wonderfully in the choir. It was greatly anointed and sang almost every service. She was greatly honored to have held this position.

I was blessed to have held various positions myself. Teaching is one of my callings, and I have done this most of my Christian life. I also have a heart for missions. Though I have never been on a mission's trip, I have always felt the need to support those who do mission's work and are on the mission field.

As I have just stated, one of my callings is to teach. I tried to use this calling in the men's prayer meeting and men's singles' group to help get other Christian men established in the ways of God. God would move greatly in these meetings. One night, we men were gathered in the basement. We laid hands on a brother, and the power of God came down like it did in the Bible. It fell on all of us, and we began to speak in other tongues as the Spirit gave us utterance. We were all drunk in the Spirit to one degree or another. One brother drove home with the Spirit all over him, and his wife had to help him into the house. It's amazing that God can fill you in that way. We had many services like that.

In 1999, God led us out of Union Hill. It was hard to leave, but God always has a plan. In the time that we were gone from Union Hill, we always came back for revivals and funerals. In 2004, we had a tragedy hit us like never before. We lost our twenty-five-year-old daughter, Gina, in a vehicle accident. She had accepted the Lord as her Savior before she passed away, but it was still so hard to lose her to death. Union Hill Church as well as Beechfork Church and Locust Grove Faith Community Church were instrumental in helping us through this trying time.

We lived our lives for God. We fully believed that because we were faithful to take our kids to church and to teach them the ways of

God, God moved on our daughter to bring her back to Him before she passed. She had a heart for the Lord. She had been under conviction for a while and had made up her mind that she was going to get saved. If it had not been for Union Hill teaching her as a child and us getting that teaching down inside her, she would not have known to call upon the Lord in the last moments of her life and to accept Him as her Savior.

Though we had left Union Hill Church, it always had a place in our hearts. Then in 2014, after fifteen years, God led us back. We thank the Lord for what He has done in our lives and, if the Lord tarries, are looking forward to what God is going to do at Union Hill Church in the future.

SUMMARY

After each service ends in prayer, we fellowship with one another. As we gather our personal belongings to leave the building, we shake hands and say our good-byes to various individuals with an attitude of "have a good week" and "looking forward to seeing you next service." When we walk out those doors and get in our cars to go home, it is always with the anticipation that we will soon return. Who knows what God will do in the next service?

Baby dedication

Golden Treasurers Dinner celebrating July 4th, 2009

1997 Union Hill youth

Christmas 1996

February 2003, Washington DC
Right to Life panel
Ken Johnson, Phil Fulton, and Don Swarthout

Ten Commandments crusade at Peebles High School
March 24, 2004, Washington DC
Support of our pledge of allegiance

Pastor Phil Fulton and Reverend Rob Schenck with Faith In Action

Eunice Minton

Church group

THOSE WHO HAVE
GONE ON BEFORE US

This book would not be complete if we did not mention those bastions of faith who have passed on before us in the last twenty-five years.

Phillip Lee Swayne

Phil left us at the early age of fifty-six. He left behind a legacy for his family to follow. He was faithful, kind, and a wonderful worship leader. God's anointing was upon him. Heaven has been made sweeter because of him.

Harley (Bud) and Ruby Swayne

Bud and Ruby raised their kids at Union Hill. Ruby prayed that she would have a child who would play the piano. Because of her prayers, we have her daughter, Sharon Swayne Fulton, our Pastor's wife, as our piano player. Once Bud got up and testified that he could not raise his arm to praise the Lord because it hurt so badly. On another night, the Lord told him to raise his hands and praise Him, and when he did, God healed him.

Johnny and Bessie Ward

Johnny and Bessie also raised their kids at Union Hill. So many times, Johnny got up and testified about God saving him and prayed for his kids to get saved. Bessie was quiet in church but was always there encouraging everyone else.

Bob and Eunice Minton

Bob and Eunnie were faithful to the end. Bob was quiet and played the lead guitar. When he would testify, tears would flow down his face. Eunice was our song leader. She always knew what song to sing. One night, the Spirit fell, and she and Pastor Phil held hands and danced in the Spirit on the platform. Another time, she testified that the Lord told her that her hands were like a TV antenna. She needed to get her hands up in the air to get better reception. She really got blessed that night.

Faye Thompson

What can we say about Sister Faye? She was a short, red-headed woman, who when she sang, the Spirit always fell. She sang "There Ain't No Grave," "I'm Gonna Cling," and "Who's that Yonder," just to name a few. Sometimes Faye would get to church two hours before it started.

Nanny Thompson

Nanny was a quiet lady who would sing and read poems. She had such a sweet and wonderful spirit.

Earnal and Stella Ward

Though Stella is still with us, her health keeps her from coming to church. She and Earnal were two great people who loved God and were faithful to Him and the church. Earnal served as Sunday school superintendent and a trustee for years. Though Stella was not emotional, she was one of the prettiest dancers when the Spirit got on her.

Otto and Flora Hilterbrand

Otto had one of the biggest smiles and hearts there ever was. He and Flora were faithful to God and the church. They were two of the nicest people God ever saved. They always greeted everyone with a smile, a handshake, and a hug.

Joe and Norma Jean Swayne

Joe and Norma Jean were always late but always faithful. Joe was the Sunday school treasurer for years. He was a quiet man, but when he spoke, people listened. He had a very kind and gentle spirit. Norma Jean was a prayer warrior. She spent all day going about her business and praying for everything and everyone.

Troy and Drusilla Smith

Tory and Drusilla were quiet also but faithful. Troy was a trustee for years and was on the board when we voted to build a new sanctuary. Drusilla was a beautiful, quiet woman. Both would give wonderful testimonies about what God had done for them.

Tim Adams

In 2011, Tim, at the age of fifty-two, was one of ours who was also taken too soon. He always had a happy face. He went on a missionary trip to Africa and was a powerful witness for the Lord.

Mr. and Mrs. Bob Carter

The Carters were some of the nicest people. They too were faithful to God and the church.

J. C. McCane

J. C. was another faithful and quiet one. He was always there giving.

Bill and Katherine Day

Bill was our first greeter. He would shake your hand and give you a piece of candy. He had a wonderful spirit. Katherine was a tiny woman with only a little bit of gray in her hair. When she would shout her curls would bob up and down.

Brother and Sister Dotson

Brother and Sister Dotson always sat in the fourth seat back on the left side facing the pulpit. Brother Dotson would get blessed and crawl on the floor. Sister Dotson's head would shake back and forth when she would get blessed.

Sarah Ballard

Sister Ballard never missed church until her health prevented her from coming.

Earl Howard

Brother Earl left us too soon. He never said much but was also faithful. He left us with his wonderful wife, Sister Ina, who still gives some of the best testimonies about this "Great salvation."

Jim and Virdie Grooms

Virdie didn't get saved until the 1991 revival, but everyone thought she was a Christian all those years because she never missed a service. She never professed to being a Christian though. Then one night during the revival, the Lord got ahold of her heart, and she became a new creature in Christ.

Robie and Genevieve Purdue

When Brother Robie got blessed, he would always pat his face, because when the Spirit got on him, he would go numb. Sister Genevieve would sometimes sing. One of her songs was "It's Me Again Lord." Everyone got a blessing from her.

Lee and Blanche York

Lee and Blanche started attending Union Hill right before we built the new sanctuary. Lee was hardworking and put a lot of time into the church. God used him and Blanche to help us build.

Bill and Genia Cassidy

Bill used his crane to move the wall mural from the old to the new church. His first wife passed away, and he married Genia. They were faithful to the church the rest of their lives.

Bud and Alta Ward

Bud and Alta were two very sweet people. Bud would testify and run around the altar clapping his hands. Alta was quiet but so sweet. They are missed in the church.

Louise Warnok

Louise was a sweet lady. She never missed a service until her health failed her.

Dorothy Jamison

Dorothy was also sweet and faithful.

Dick and Janet Farmer

These two also never missed church and were some of the nicest people you would ever meet.

Union Hill's Children

Last but not least are the children who were raised at Union Hill under godly teaching and whom God decided to take early in life to spend eternity with him.

Timmy Ward, who died at age thirteen and was the son of Tom and Connie Ward

Johnathan Brown, who died as a newborn and was the son of David and Lisa Brown

Regina (Gina) Smalley, who died at age twenty-five and was the daughter of Toby and Joyce Smalley

Josh Conaway, who died at age thirty-one and was the son of Mike and Anita Conaway

T. J. Green, who was the son of Ruth Pitzer and Pete Green

Brian Cluxton, who died at age nineteen and was the son of Mike and Connie Cluxton

Billy Dale Purtee, who died at the age of thirty-two and was the son of Bob and Rita Purtee.

We do not understand the ways of the Lord, but His ways are higher than our ways. By the grace of God, you have made it home and we will see you again.

Bob and Eunice Minton

Faye Thompson

Earnal and Stella Ward

Troy and Drusilla Smith

Mr. and Mrs. Bob Carter

J. C. McCane

Sara Ballard and her brother Virgil

Jim and Verdi Grooms

Genia Cassidy

Verdi Grooms and her brother Joe Swayne

Troy Smith, Bud Swayne, Drusilla Smith, and Carey Hilderbran

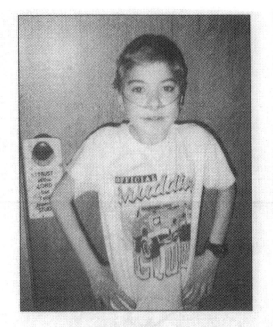

This book is dedicated to the memory of
Timothy Joe Ward
March 17, 1979 - August 24, 1992

Timmy was diagnosed with cystic fibrosis when he was only a few weeks old. Timmy loved the Lord. Many times when entering his room, you could find Tim on his knees talking to the Lord. He attended a public school until his health no longer allowed him to. He loved Sunday School and always had good things to say about his teachers. Timmy was a faithful member of Union Hill Church. Thank you, Lord, for letting us have him for 13 years and 7 months.

Timmy Ward

Regina "Gina" Smalley

Josh Conaway

Billy Dale Purtee

POSITIONS HELD AT UNION HILL CHURCH

MINISTRIES

Music Ministries

Song Leader
Eunice Mitton, 1991

Choir Director
Joyce Smalley, 1992 to 1999
Philip Lee Swayne, 1999 to 2015
Norman (Bud) Brabson 2015 to present

Worship Leader
Philip Lee Swayne, 1999 to 2015
Norman (Bud) Brabson, 2015 to the present

Men's Prayer Meeting Leader
Toby Smalley
First men's prayer meeting was on Wednesday, April 29, 1992. Then it moved to Monday nights. Later, it was moved to every other Sunday at 5 p.m.

Women's Prayer Meeting/Women's Ministries
Judy Kay Van Hoy, 1991 to 2016

Christmas sharing was started as part of home missions under missionary leader Toby Smalley in 1996. Then it was moved to be part of the Sunday school.

The clothing drive was after the 1997 flood.

Lists of Positions

Pastors
Phil Fulton, 1991 to present

Church Secretary
Judy Ann Ward, 1991 to present

First Elder
Harley (Bud) Swayne, 1991 to 1992
Norman (Bud) Brabson, 1992 to 2001
Dennis Ward, 2001 to 2007
Philip Lee Swayne, 2008 to 2015
Norman (Bud) Brabson, 2015 to present

Trustees
Earnel Ward, 1991 to 1999
Troy Smith, 1991 to 1992
Walter VanHoy, 1991 to 1994
Keith Spriggs, 1991 to 1999
Tim Howe, 1996 to 2010
Ronnie Anderson, 1999 to 2002
Keith Ward, 1991 to 2008
Bobbie Minton, 1994 to present
Jeff Cutler, 2002 to present
Teresa Ball, 2006 to present
Judy Ann Ward, 2010 to present
Ronnie Shriver, 2014 to present

Young People's Leader

Judy Kay Van Hoy, 1991 to 1996 (1993 to 1994, position was shared by Judy Kay VanHoy and Tim Adams)
Keith and Brenda Spriggs, 1996 to 1997
Lee York, 1997 to 1998
Toby Smalley, 1998
Tessa Swayne, 1999 to 2002

Young People's Leader (Position name revised to Preteen and Teen Leaders)
Preteen Leader

Tessa Swayne, 2002 to present

Teen Leader

Wendy (VanHoy) Purden, 2002 to 2010
Tina Fulton, 2010 to 2015
Nathan and Amy Smalley, 2016 to present

Missionary Leader

Toby Smalley, 1991 to 1998
Amber (Knauff) Fergusson, 1998 to 1999
Alton Swayne, 1999 to 2000
Judy Kay VanHoy, 2000 to present

Janitors for the Church

Joyce Smalley
Ruth Pitzer
Stan and Kay Helton
Alton and Mary Swayne
Lee Ann Ward
Rita Purtee

Janitors for the Community Center

Stan and Kay Helton
Gerry and Diane Perry

Keith and Judy Ward
Dan and Sherry Gammon

Sunday School Superintendent
Earnel Ward
Tim Howe
Lisa Howe
Lisa Brown/Jeff Cutler

Sunday School Treasurer/Secretary
Joe Swayne, 1991 to 1997
Tonya Swayne, 1997 to present

Sunday School Teachers (not in any particular order)
Tonya Swayne
Lisa Brown
Christine Brabson
Amy Swayne
Beth Aber
Kim Swayne
Tessa Swayne
Teresa Shriver
Brenda Springs
Alton Swayne
Lisa Howe
Brian Fulton
Toby Smalley
Lee York
Judy Kay VanHoy
Tom Smith
Naomi Russell
Tammy Atkins
Nathan Smalley
Amy Smalley
Keith Spriggs

Scott Russell
Tim Howe
Bud Brabson
Judy Ann Ward
Phil Fulton

Assistant Sunday School Teachers (not in any particular order)

Teresa Shriver
Amy Swayne
Beth Aber
Ruthie Pitzer
Penny Hibbs
Brenda Farmer
Teresa Ball
Amber Ferguson
Daniel Ferguson
Linda Purdue
Carol Snively
Betty Shriver
Kim Browning
Carol Anderson
Tim Adams
Mary Swayne
Lisa Howe
Naomi Russell
Karelen Leonard
Jeff Swayne
Lisa Brown
Alan Seitz
Shirley Karns
Scott Russell
Kathy Finlaw
Elly Kelly
Randy Ball
Ronnie Anderson

Chris Allred
Tim Howe
Jeff Cutler
Bobby Minton

Printed in the United States
By Bookmasters